INDIAN WOMEN TODAY

Indian Women Today

GIRIJA KHANNA

MARIAMMA A. VARGHESE

VIKAS PUBLISHING HOUSE PVT LTD
New Delhi Bombay Bangalore Calcutta Kanpur

VIKAS PUBLISHING HOUSE PVT LTD
5 Ansari Road, New Delhi 110002
Savoy Chambers, 5 Wallace Street, Bombay 400001
10 First Main Road, Gandhi Nagar, Bangalore 560009
8/1-B Chowringhee Lane, Calcutta 700016
80 Canning Road, Kanpur 208004

ISBN 0 7069 0679 9

1V02K3801

Printed at Roopak Printers, K-17 Navin Shahdara, Delhi-110032

Preface

The fervour created during the International Women's Year has
abated, but the problems of women have not thereby disappeared.
They remain as intense as ever. Surely, the idea of the International
Women's Year was not to bring a miraculous cure within a year
for all the social evils that women are made to face in a male
dominated society. It was more to arouse consciousness among all
sections of the people about women, their problems, and the possible remedies for them. International Women's Year has created a
universal awareness of women's problems to a considerable degree
and now is the time for intense follow up, careful study, and
assessment of women and their problems.

In India, as in any other country, the problems a woman faces
have a specific colouring depending on the socio-economic-cultural
milieu in which she has been nurtured and moulded. Her problems
are influenced by various social considerations and she and her life
necessarily determine the welfare of the home, family and society.
Hence, towards understanding woman's problems what would be
the first step? One has to know her in the context of her home,
family, work and community.

Inspired by this purpose, we ventured on this elaborate study to
find out her role as a wife, a mother, a working person; her views
on sex, marriage and family planning; on adoption, fashion,
religion, politics etc. and thereby help a clearer picture to emerge.

Where does today's woman stand in the social structure of
modern India? What has been the change in her in the last three
decades? In what areas is she reluctant to change? What is her

psychological attitude to change? Until these are known any assessment of Indian women and their problems would be incomplete.

These are some of the questions we have tried to answer in this book, which is the first joint effort by a doctor and an educationist to study Indian women. This gave us the advantage of establishing better rapport with the respondents, especially when discussing personal details. This book is the outcome of face-to-face discussions we have had with a sample of one thousand Indian women selected at random from all socio-economic strata, and it took us about two years to collect and compile the data. We wished to complete the book during the Women's International Year but the voluminous data and its analysis took two more years to complete.

You will read here what opinions the doe-eyed Bengali daughter-in-law has about a joint family, why the South Indian "Mami" vehemently advocates sex education for her granddaughter, why a cobbler's wife took to prostitution, or why a Gujarati doctor's widow chose to live with her brother-in-law instead of remarrying. This spectrum of human experiences portrays the Indian woman in all her aspects.

As statistical figures are indispensable for any scientific work, our study is primarily based on the data collected from the questionnaire. To make each interview as comprehensive as possible we used the "open ended" questionnaire in which rigid ticking of answers was replaced by an elaborate interview giving each respondent every opportunity to speak in a natural, uninhibited way. Even the order of questions had often to be changed to keep up the continuity of thought. Often much more than what was contained in the questionnaire was discussed, as in the case of a middle-aged housewife in Allahabad who came up with many personal details about her married life which were shocking even to us.

It would have been impracticable to put in the book all the thousand case studies collected by us, although each one of them was interesting. However we have incorporated some of them to bring out the true picture and make the book interesting for the non-specialist reader.

GIRIJA KHANNA
MARIAMMA A. VARGHESE

Contents

ONE

Introduction

A proper assessment of Indian women today necessarily involves a brief resumé of the cultural background of Indian women through the ages. Unlike her western counterpart the Indian woman is part of a culture which goes a back into the past. If she has a particular conviction or acts in a specific manner it is due to the pattern that has been ingrained in her by the fairly stable social structure of a thousand years.

The highest place has been accorded to woman in Indian religious and philosophical thought. The primordial one is conceived as a harmony of *purusha* (male) and *prakriti* (female). The concept of *ardhanariswara* describes god-head as half female and half male. The Shakti cult is centred around the superiority and destructive strength of the female. Rivers and streams, dawn and twilight, flowers and seasons, knowledge and music are conceived of as feminine. The elevation of the feminine principle pervades Vedic thought. The social structure in the Vedic period admitted the equality of woman. Hymn XXI of The *Rig Veda* extols the virtues of women as even greater than those of men.

Throughout the Vedic period woman was given a status equal to man's to participate in sacrificial rites, to undergo the investituer ceremony, and to be man's equal in upholding "dharma". She could fight wars, join in festivals, take part in philosophical discussions, like Gargi and Maitreye, or even remain unmarried if she so desired.

In the latter part of the Vedic period the law maker Gautama described eight different kinds of marriage, giving latitude in the choice of spouse both to men and women. Inter-caste marriages were permitted. The lower the caste, the more liberal were the rules. A girl who was not given in marriage at the proper age had the liberty to choose her own life partner.

Widow remarriage by the *niyoga* form was permitted whereby a widow could wed her brother-in-law or a man belonging to her husband's caste. This, however, was more to maintain the family institution than as a special licence for the sex life for a widow.

With the passage of time there was a gradual degradation in woman's status. During the next period, from 200 BC to 200 AD, which would come under the Smrita period, the most significant law maker was Manu. His social codes and sanctions left their marks permanently on the future status of the Indian woman. Manu clamped down woman's freedom in certain spheres in order to safeguard her position and to preserve the family structure.

Manu's famous dictum "a woman must be her father's shadow in childhood, her husband's in her youth, her son's in old age" is too well known. But Manu was not a woman hater, for it was Manu who said, "Where women are honoured there the gods are pleased, where they are not honoured no sacred rites yield rewards."

Manu vehemently opposed the purchase of a woman. He never gave legal sanction to such a marriage. He recognised the adoption of a girl as *putrika* which conferred on her all the rights of a son. Manu brought down the age of marriage for a girl and advocated child marriage, though he warned fathers not to give away their daughters to men devoid of good qualities.

Though polygamy was practiced, he strongly advocated monogamy and attached the greatest improtance to sexual restraint and fidelity to one's spouse. He laid down different rules even for a man contemplating separation. A woman deserted by her husband was given the right to marry after the lapse of a certain number of years. Thus Manu stood as the principal law maker of the conservative Hindu period. His prime objective was to safeguard the interests of the family and society at the expense of individual liberty.

In the period that followed, Manu had to put further restrictions on women. As the whole of northern India from the Punjab to the Indo-Gangetic Plain was subjected to repeated foreign invasions by the Aryans, the Huns, the Arabs, the Melianisians and others, the security of women was seriously jeopardised as they were often carried away by the invading races. Woman, instead of being an asset to the family, became a liability. Child-marriage became the rule rather than the exception.

The advent of Buddhism saw a welcome change in women's position in society. It allowed women the freedom to be educated, to travel as missionaries or even to remain unmarried. But it also considered woman an evil to be avoided by men. This was probably due to the austere measures of the Buddhist high priests for their menfolk. The Jataka tales are full of long passages describing the evil and vile nature of women.

The situation changed for the worse with the Muslim invasion in the eleventh century. Life became insecure. Woman were forcibly taken away to be slaves or to marry into Muslim homes. The consequent insecurity and instability further narrowed down a woman's social liberties. But even in this period, magnanimity was shown to women made "impure" by the invaders, and rules were laid down to retrieve women who were abducted.

Social sanction for the self immolation of widows came in. Before this period *sati* and *anumaranam* did occur off and on but not as a regular feature. As a result of repressive social and religious custom, a woman sometimes even preferred *sati* to widowhood. Though there were schools which strongly opposed *sati* for the average woman, the *summum bonum* of a woman's life was to marry, live for her husband and family and die with him. However, parts of India not affected by Muslim invasions remained practically free from the evils of *purdah, sati* and female infanticide.

India has been the crucible for different ethnic groups and varied cultures. Each alien influence has left its mark on the people of the land. Even if the cultural habits and practices of the alien invading group were not absorbed *in toto*, there was a considerable exchange of ideas and practices which influenced and modified what already existed.

In the eighteenth century, at the dawn of British rule, the position of women in India was in a sorry state. The Vedic liberties enjoyed by women were forgotten. Only the fossilised narrow practices of a conservative, static society prevailed. The British government's attitude of non-interference with the religious sentiments of the local people stopped all social reforms for a century. However, due to the pioneering work of some leaders, changes were brought about in the social structure of the country in the later part of the nineteenth century. Legal sanctions were given for the removal of caste disabilities, widow remarriage, women's right to property etc. But conservative Indians were not willing to accept these social reforms because they were initiated by an alien government. In spite of the legal sanctions for their removal many of the old practices continued.

After centuries of social stagnation, due to a combination of divergent factors, social, cultural, economic and political, Indian woman showed a sudden urge to come back into the mainstream of social life. The first impetus was given by the freedom movement. This marked the beginning of a new era for Indian women.

Even though the number of women actively drawn out of their homes into the freedom movement was negligible in comparison with the millions living in the towns and villages throughout the length and breadth of the country, this return into community life was a significant factor in shaping the future of Indian women.

Under the inspiration of great political leaders, women stepped on to the streets to join hands with men to carry out *satyagraha* or go behind bars. The nonviolent character of the freedom struggle appealed to the innate nature of women and they willingly responded to the call. This desire to be part of the changes taking place in the country was a great comeback for the Indian woman for it helped her to re-attain her rightful place.

With independence, women were granted equal status with men. The government made an all-out effort to raise the status of women in the various fields through legislation. Compulsory education, the Hindu Marriage Act, raising of the marriageable age, the Adoption Act, dowry prohibition, and the legalising of abortion are all in favour of women. But the law alone is not enough to bring about a radical change. A change has to come in the attitudes of men and women. If the country has to progress unimpeded, women, who form one half of the population, must cast off the shackles of social taboos, superstitions and ignorance and become equal partners with men in shaping free India.

Generally speaking men and women want to live up to the expectations of society. In a nascent democracy healthy new trends have to be set which will decide the country's future. Educated women have to make full use of all the social privileges and set new trends for the masses to follow. This will revitalise the social position of Indian women and, through them, the country.

The next ten years will be a crucial period in the history of our nation. It is of the utmost importance to assess the emerging Indian woman in terms of her status, her various roles, and her aspirations to know the direction in which she is moving.

The purpose of the present investigation was to study the status of women today and their role in the family and society in general. The study is divided into several broad areas of investigation like Indian women, their aspirations, employment, marriage and marital adjustment, sex life, family planning, parent-daughter relationship, fashion, recreation, and other social and economic aspects of their lives.

SAMPLING DESIGN

The nature of information required in this investigation is very personal and hence it was essential to establish rapport with the respondents of the study. Attempts were made to get a representative sample of Indian women from different areas of the country and belonging to different socio-economic strata. The classification of the states into five different zones, East, West, South, North and Central according to *India 1971-72* published by the Information and Broadcasting Bureau was adopted.

To select the families, a two stage probability sampling design was adopted. Areas of the country formed the first stage unit. The sample households, belonging to the three socio-economic status, formed the second stage unit. A pooled sample was generated from the five different areas with the three sub-samples which would give valid estimates for different strata and also of the sample as a whole. Altogether 1000 women were interviewed, 200 from each of the five areas. From each area, 50 women each from the upper and lower socio-economic group and 100 from the middle socio-economic group have been included in making up a complete sample.

The women were selected at random from different localities in chosen cities from each area. The colonies belonging to upper, middle, and lower socio-economic strata were approached. The authors' fluency in Hindi and five other Indian languages made interviewing the women from different areas and socio-economic groups comparatively easy. The cities selected for the study were

Calcutta, Cuttack, Gauhati, Darjeeling, Ranchi, Allahabad, Lucknow, Delhi, Jaipur, Ahmedabad, Bombay, Nagpur, Madras, Bangalore, Trivandrum, and Kottayam.

The socio-economic strata was identified by the Kuppuswami scale with modifications of the family income scale as recommended by the National Applied Economic Council. A composite score for income, education, and occupation was obtained which was further classified into three groups of upper, middle, and lower socio-economic classes. Of the women who were contacted, only the healthy and those who were willing to respond to the questions were selected. Although the demographic figures for India show the broad base of the poorer section of the society, it was decided to take only 25% of the sample from this category because their views might be restricted because of imperfect education and limited exposure to the outside world. The upper socio-economic group was also represented by 25% of the sample. More weight-age was given to the middle socio-economic group as this group was expected to respond with a wider perspective of the issues involved.

CHARACTERISTICS OF THE SAMPLE

The sample is comprised of equal numbers of women from each of the five areas. Different religious groups, like Hindus, Muslims, Sikhs, Christians and others were included in approximate proportion to their representation in the country. Different communities were represented from each area. For example the Eastern zone was represented by the Bengalis, Biharis, Assamese, Oriyas; the West was represented by the Maharashtrians, Gujaratis, Parsis, Khojas and Goans; the South consisted of the Malayalis, Tamilians, Kanaries and Telugus; the North comprised the Punjabis, Kashmiris, Rajasthanis, Sikhs, and Sindhis; and the Central zone was represented by women from Uttar Pradesh and Madhya Pradesh.

Table 1

CHARACTERISTICS OF THE SAMPLE

Age Groups	Frequency	Percentage
15-24	231	23.10
25-34	390	39.00
35-44	264	26.40
More than 45	115	11.50
Total	1,000	100.00
Marital status		
Married	780	78.00
Unmarried	139	13.90
Widowed	52	5.20
Divorced	29	2.90
Total	1,000	100.00
Education		
Illiterate	127	12.70
Primary school	126	12.60
Middle school	95	9.50
High school	166	16.60
Intermediate	136	13.60
College	296	29.60
Professional training	54	5.40
Total	1,000	100.00
Type of family		
Nuclear family	627	62.70
Joint family	373	37.30
Total	1,000	100.00
Occupational structure		
Housewife	646	64.60
Working wife	203	20.30
Single working woman	55	5.50
Student	80	8.00
Student wife	16	1.60
Total	1,000	100.00

The majority of women in the sample belong to the 25-34 age group and more than 75% of the sample were married. About half of them had less than high school education and the other half had college education, some with advanced professional training. The majority of the women were housewives and only 20% of them were working. About 66% of them lived in nuclear families.

COLLECTION OF DATA

An interview schedule was constructed to include all aspects of the study. During the open ended interviews women spoke in confidence to a professional doctor. This facilitated not only greater rapport but greater reliability and authenticity in the responses collected. Respondents were encouraged to speak freely on each aspect which seemed relevant to the subject under investigation. They were assured that individual responses would be kept confidential, and in case studies only fictitious names would be used. Each of the respondents was questioned about the various topics mentioned below though not necessarily in the order presented.

(*i*) *Situational Characteristics*. State of origin, religion, type of family, age, marital status, total family income, husband's/father's occupation, husband's/father's education, education/occupation, size of family of orientation, ordinal position, parent's married life.

(*ii*) *Marriage and Married Life*. Age at marriage, ideal age for marriage, age difference between husband and wife, ideal age difference between husband and wife, type of marriage, preference for the type of marriage, courtship pattern, selected characteristics for a marriage partner, self-evaluation of married life, marital adjustment and maladjustment, factors relating to marital happines.

(*iii*) *Sex and Family Planning*. Attitude towards sex, sexual frequency, sexual satisfaction, sex knowledge before marriage, discussing sex with husband and friends, family planning.

(*iv*) *Socio-economic and Cultural Aspects of Family Life*. Familial roles of women, task differentiation between husband and wife, role in decision making, type of family, type of family preferred, size of the family and the preferred family size, living with children in old age, consumer responsibilities, saving pattern, political interests, personalities admired, importance of religion, frequency of visiting places of worship, observing fasts and keeping a shrine at home, belief in spiritual guide, social service, recreation and entertainment.

(*v*) *Parent-daughter Relationship*. Interactional problems with parents, change in outlook between parents and daughters, abiding by the wishes of parents, socialisation of daughters, girls' education, extra training for girls, sex education for girls, restriction imposed by parents.

(*vi*) *Fashion*. Fashion consciousness, choice of dress, preference for unconventional dress, use of lipstick, fashion ideas, smoking, drinking and tranquillisers.

(*vii*) *Social Practices and Issues*. Inter-caste marriage, attitude towards, dowry, divorce, widow remarriage, adoption, co-education, sexual freedom, premarital sex.

(*viii*) *Employment of Women*. Attitude towards employment of married women, why there is objection to the employment of married women, why married women work, effects of employment on married women, preference for the type of jobs.

Based on the information collected, data were fed into an IBM 1401 computer to find out the frequency and distribution of the different variables concerned and also to identify the various relationships. The findings of these are presented in the following chapters.

TWO

Marriage and Married Life

Marriage as an institution has existed in every form of society from time immemorial. Whether marriage was considered a magic ritual, a religious sacrament, or a legal contract, it has been recognised to serve certain basic functions. Marriage regulated by customs, beliefs, traditions and social laws provides for the care and upbringing of children, and gives the progeny legal recognition and social status. It makes the division of work convenient for the upkeep of the home and family, provides sexual gratification for the partners, and helps in the economic growth and welfare of society. In short, marriage caters to the very basic needs of men and women by providing security, companionship, and stability, forming the nucleus of family life. Marriage thus becomes vital for human happiness.

No wonder marriage is given the most important place in the structure of any social group, and of all the Hindu sacraments, it is the most important. The marriage ritual in India has retained its basic form and content through the ages, as the changes in the concept of Hindu marriage have been minimal in the last three thousand years.

The western idea of marriage, though originally shaped by the Greek, Roman, Hebrew, and Christian traditions, underwent a catastrophic change with the industrial revolution and again after World Wars I and II. It has come to mean a legal contract which sanctions the union of a man and a woman for personal gratification. The traditional, religious, biological and sociological aspects of marriage have been subordinated to the sole view of enhancing individual pleasure. This, unfortunately, has shaken the very foundation of domestic happiness and stability. In many parts of the world, the making and termination of marriage has become very easy depending purely on the whims and fancies of individuals.

In India, however, marriage has retained its sanctity and purity. It usually follows an endogamous caste pattern, is mostly monogamous, and continues to be a religious sacrament which brings man and woman into a life-long partnership. Polygamy, though occasionally practised, does not get social, legal, and religious sanction. Widow marriage is rare for similar reasons. The concept of *pativrata* (devotion to one husband) and *aka patni* (one wife) are deep rooted traditional convictions which time has found difficult to erase. Marriage has thus retained its religious sanctity as a life-long partnership to safeguard jointly the interests of the family, *dharma* (duty), *artha* (material prosperity) and *kama* (pleasure) being the three pivots that uphold the marriage partnership. Greater weightage is given to duty than to material wealth or sexual pleasure.

The Indian concept of marriage gives ample scope to the husband and wife to fulfil their duties to the home, family, and community. As *dampati* the husband and wife become the joint heads of the household.

The patriarchal traditions of Hindu society naturally gave the husband greater authority and power as the bread-earner and provider, with the wife becoming the nucleus of the home. She enjoyed respect and many privileges as the mother, the caretaker of the children, and the upholder of the family tradition.

Though the wife wielded less power in the economic and material sense, she was the spiritual force behind the domestic peace and integrity of the home. In a primarily agricultural society, woman became more or less an equal partner to man because of her participation and contribution to the economy of the community. True, woman occupied a different status to that of man, but she did command very many privileges in her own right as wife and mother. Her importance for domestic prosperity and community welfare was recognised and accepted. The last three decades have registered numerous reforms under the Hindu Marriage Act. Widow marriage is approved, polygamy has become illegal, inter-caste marriage is recognised, divorce has been made easier, and the age of marriage has been raised. In spite of these legal reforms, Indian marriage has not shown any radical change. It is mostly arranged within the caste, is fairly stable, monogamous, and performed according to religious rites.

In every marriage, the first few years after marriage are the most crucial in determining whether the marriage partnership will work—whether the woman will adjust to her new environment, whether emotionally she is prepared to live through the marriage partnership, whether the couple is temperamentally and sexually compatible, whether the wife can adjust with other family members, and if she has scope to pursue her individual interests in the new set up.

After marriage the Indian woman moves to her husband's home. If the husband is working and staying in a different town, city or village, she goes with him to live where he works. If he is living with his parents in a joint family then she moves into that household. In either case the wife enters the husband's environment. Only in exceptional cases does the husband stay in the wife's parental home. This happens occasionally when the wife is the only child of her parents or when the son-in-law enters his father-in-law's business. But, as in most instances the woman moves into her husband's house, the adjustment she makes after marriage is much greater than what he has to make. She moves into a new home, a new environment, to live with people she hardly knows.

The Indian girl is tutored to play her role as wife and mother from a very young age. Sooner or later she knows she has to fall in line with her mother and grandmother, get married, have a home and family and play her role as a responsible housewife. The prime ambition of even educated women is to finish their studies and settle in marriage. If a woman is not married, it is more often because she has missed her chances rather than due to a deliberate desire to remain a spinster or a liberated and economically independent female.

For an average Indian female, marriage is the most satisfying and fulfilling aspect of her life. Partly due to tradition and convention, and partly due to her own inner urge and a conviction which grows in a stable and emotionally secure upbringing, she enters marriage willingly with the positive view of making a happy home with the man she marries.

Every other consideration is subordinated to the idea of making a secure and stable husband-wife partnership. So naturally, in spite of adjustment problems, the great majority of Indian women manage to create a fairly happy marriage. Recently a professor of social studies from a foreign university commented that young girls in his country were trained and prepared to play every role other than that of wife and mother. In India, whatever a woman may or may not know, she knows how to be a wife and mother.

A great deal can be understood about a woman from her ideas on marriage, her marital happiness or otherwise, factors that decide her happiness in marriage, the usual adjustment problems she faces after marriage, causes of maladjustment, her views on sex, family life and family size. Answers to these queries will decide a woman's status in the home and family, and her position in society.

AGE AT MARRIAGE

Over 90% of Indian women are married before the age of 25. The great majority of the less educated get married when they are below 16 to 20 years old. However, the age of marriage increases with education in every socio-economic strata, and most significantly in the higher and middle socio-economic groups.

When a woman is better educated she probably belongs to a more progressive family which values women's education and is in less of a hurry to get the girls married at an early age. If a girl enters college, she is keen to finish the course she has started on and only in rare cases does she interrupt her studies to settle in marriage. Another likely reason why the age of marriage increases with education is that better educated girls become more selective. They conform less easily to traditional patterns. They prefer to marry only if they approve of a person, even if their elders have already made a selection. They would prefer to wait and marry someone they like rather than just marry for the sake of marrying. Finally, when a girl goes in for a professional course or postgraduate training it becomes difficult to find a marriage partner with an equal or better educational status. This problem increases if rigid caste restrictions are also observed or when the family is not very well off financially and unable to lure boys into marriage.

Vasantha Chettiar's case study is illustrative of this point. She belongs to the conservative Chettiar community of South India. Her father, who retired as a railway officer, gave a good education to all his four childern. Vasantha got admission into the medical

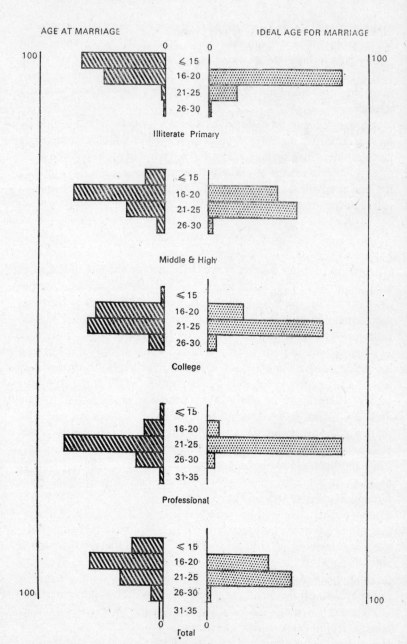

AGE AT MARRIAGE

IDEAL AGE FOR MARRIAGE

Illiterate Primary

Middle & High

College

Professional

Total

Fig. 1. Age at marriage and ideal age for marriage in relation to
educational level.

college and completed her course. Her parents started looking for a matrimonial match while she was yet a house surgeon. Somehow she couldn't find anyone suitable and Vasantha joined the M.D. course.

By this time Vasantha was over 24. After her father's retirement, her parents settled in their ancestral home near Chettinad. It became more and more difficult for them to find a suitable boy for her in the conservative environment where they lived. She had neither the determination nor the initiative to find a match of her own choice. So she decided to give up the idea of marriage and continued her post-graduate studies. Vasantha is now over 36 years old. She is working in one of the district hospitals in Tamil Nadu and has no plans to marry.

Ideas about marriage change with better education. When women were asked about the ideal age of marriage the answers showed a definite shift to a higher age bracket with better education. The most favoured age of marriage was between 20 to 25 years. The reasons given were numerous. Many women felt that girls in their early twenties would be better suited mentally and physically to take the responsibilities and strains of married life. Most girls finished graduation not before 19 or 20. The ideal time for marriage they felt was after graduation. Even if girls went in for some technical or secretarial course after schooling they could have a few years of fruitful employment before marriage.

Malathi, a U.P. bank clerk's wife vehemently asserted, "I married at 15 and see what has become of me at 35 after six child births and a large family to take care of! I would never want my daughters to be married so early. My two girls are in high school. They will finish B.A. at least before marriage so that they will be qualified to take up a job if necessary."

Most of the educated women felt that the preferable age limit for marriage should be below 25. After this age, adjustment to a new way of life in a different home becomes very difficult. The charm of marrying fairly young and raising a family is lost when the couples are too old. Besides, the chances of marriage also become less as the age of a girl goes beyond 25. Instances were cited of women who delayed marriage on some pretext or other and later never got married.

It is interesting to note that middle-class professional women stand apart in opting for a higher age bracket for marriage as com-

pared to professionals in a higher socio-economic strata. This may
be so because women of the middle socio-economic class, once they
go in for a professional course, become more career oriented than
their counterparts in the higher class. Women from the middle
classes are more particular about completing their professional
training before marriage. They also feel more responsible about
their marriages than women of the higher classes who know that
their parents are well off and therefore can give them a good education and spend on their marriage also.

Hemlata, the daughter of an accountant, married after completing her M. Com. and working for 6 years in a bank. Since her
parents could only afford either to educate her or get her married,
she let her parents know that she would save for her marriage once
she had a job. Hemlata emphasised, "A girl can be responsible for
her marriage only if she works for a few years before settling down.
I am proud to tell you that every rupee that was spent in my
marriage was what I had saved from my salary. It is very unfair to
expect our parents to give us a good education and then pay a
handsome dowry to get a husband. My brothers have now nothing
to grumble about."

When education is not considered, women belonging to all socio-
economic groups prefer a younger age for marriage. "In big cities
a woman's ways get corrupted if they are not married at the proper age", explained Mrs Prabhu. "Hence early marriage, between
16 to 18 years, is best for women, otherwise they go astray." It
was commonly held that adjusting to a new life after marriage is
easy if the girl was below 20. "There is a wider choice of grooms
if the girl is still in her teens", "it is better to marry off a girl before
she develops preconveived notions about marriage", and "half the
charm of married life is lost if women are far too mature", were
some of the other opinions expressed.

Women of a low socio-economic strata are naturally conservative
in their views on marriage as their level of education is very low.
Menoka Nuskar, a maid servant, seemed surprised that women
should delay marriage. For her, the time a girl came of age, say
13 or 14, was ripe for marriage. After this maybe for a year or
two marriage could be postponed for financial stringency, health
reasons, or even the education of the girl. But beyond that she saw
no sense in postponing marriage for girls. "It is alright for rich
people to keep grown up daughters in the house without getting

them married, but not for poor people like us. From the time a girl becomes 'siyani' till she is married, she is a big responsibility for her mother and father. Why delay marriage? We do not want to see our girls go astray. Besides no one will marry them if they

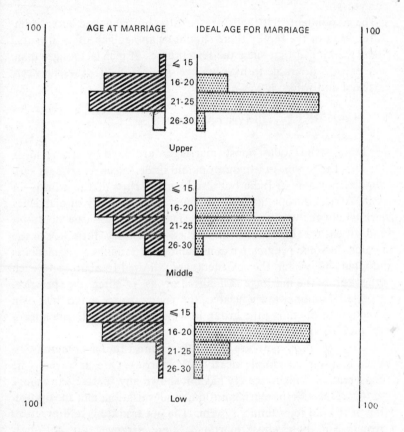

Fig. 2. Age at marriage and ideal age for marriage in relation to socio-economic status.

are not married off at the proper young age." Many other women from a low economic group expressed more or less the same views. "A girl must be married when she matures and becomes a woman," they asserted.

The respondents were asked about the age difference between themselves and their husbands. Slightly more than 40% had an age difference ranging from 5-10 years. Over 30% had a difference of less than 5 years. The same respondents were asked about the ideal age difference between husband and wife. 54% of them prefer an age difference of 5-10, while 45% prefer a difference of less than five years.

The respondents felt that to respect the husband and accept him as the head of the family there should be an age gap of 5-10 years. Some mentioned that since the sexual urges of men last longer than women, it is desirable to have an age gap of 5-10 years between husband and wife.

TYPE OF MARRIAGE

In India, even today most marriages are fixed by arrangement between the families of the groom and bride. Such marriages are popular not only in India but also in many parts of the world—in Asia, Africa, Europe, and South America. A majority of marriages throughout the world are arranged. The families do the selection and often the individuals concerned have very little say in the matter. In some progressive communities or families a via media is adopted by which the partners are allowed to approve of each other before the marriage is finalised or as is often the practice, especially among the educated, the young people make their own selection from among the group in which they mix with the approval and blessings of their parents.

Arranged marriages are the rule in most Indian communities. Even in an urban sample, nearly 90% marriages are arranged. The conservative Indian society has not shown any spectacular change in this respect despite urbanisation, modernisation, and the uprooting of the old joint family system. The old traditions and practices remain, and those whose marriages were arranged do not show any inclination towards love marriage. They are convinced that old is gold and there is no need to adopt a new method which gives greater freedom to individuals. Over 88% of women whose marriage were arranged prefer the old system, and only 11% of them recommend love marriage. On the other hand, among those who married for love, 80% prefer a love marriage and over 19% said they were in favour of an arranged match (as seen in Table 2).

Table 2

TYPES OF MARRIAGE AND PREFERENCES

Preference	Arranged Marriage		Love Marriage	
	No.	%	No.	%
Arranged	680	88.40	22	19.13
Love	89	11.60	93	80.87
Total	769	100.00	115	100.00

This finding clearly reveals that women whose marriages were arranged are surer of the advantages of such a match than women who married for love are of love marriages, which sometimes create greater adjustment problems and insecurity. The All India Women's Conference, in a meeting held in Calcutta in 1977, made a statement suggesting that love marriages often result in broken homes because of improper selection of partners without any mature judgement. The boy selected might not have a proper job to support the family or the girl might not have a background comparable to the boys, which could be factors resulting in separation.

Those who agreed to arranged marriages felt that these promise greater stability. Numerous examples were given of love marriages ending unhappily. As an arranged match is more easily accepted by the families of the husband and wife, the marriage creates a stable home and a better environment for children to grow up in. Kamini Shah, a Gujarati businessman's wife, was convinced that in the long run arranged matches were happier. She substantiated her opinion by saying, "After all in India even today, marriage is the coming together of two families. A marriage has to be planned, arranged, and made fully acceptable, not only to a man and a woman but to the families to which they belong. Love may be allright for some time but marriage is for a lifetime. Only an arranged match can give this strength to marriage."

Padma Nair did not approve of love marriage as it usually affected traditional or individual values and made it difficult for others in the family to marry. She cited the example of her brother who married an Ezhava girl. Because of it, both her marriage and that of her sister's were delayed.

Mrs Singh, a music teacher, who had a love marriage herself, preferred an arranged marriage. "My husband is from U.P. and I am from Punjab. We were neighbours before marriage. During the three years of courtship I never realised men could be so jealous. As I did not have a traditional match within my community my husband now feels that my morals must have been loose. What surprises me is that he never thought of this when he was courting me and finally decided to marry me." Most women spoke from their own personal experiences.

Mrs Ganguly, a South Indian married to a Bengali sales representative, recommended arranged marriages although she had a love marriage herself. "I would never want my daughter to have a love match. The in-laws will never respect a woman who falls in love and marries. I feel so isolated because of my marriage. I have neither the love of my husband's people nor the sympathy of my own parents. If for some reason my marriage fails, I will have no one to whom I can go. Love marriage may be fine when a woman is educated and employed but not for typical housewives like me." This throws light on the Indian woman's dependence on her parental family for support in dealing with personal crises.

Most women who had opted for a love marriage felt it was essential to know the man properly before marriage. "It is inconceivable that one could spend a lifetime with a man one does not even know," was Miss Mittal's remark. Some progressive mothers said it matters very little if a marriage is arranged or for love as long as the man is a nice person, well placed, and with a good family background.

Mrs Prasad from U. P. felt that the time has gone when parents could arrange a marriage for a boy or girl. Her own daughter, working in a foreign embassy, married a Christian boy. She felt that working men and women were old enough to choose their own life partners without bothering their parents.

Type of Marriage in Working and Non-Working Women

Over 90% of housewives had arranged marriages while only 74% of working women had conventional arranged matches (Fig. 3.). The reasons why a greater number of working women (nearly 25%) gravitate towards love matches could be numerous. As they are working, and probably better educated, their outlook on marriage changes. Because they have greater opportunity to meet men at the place of work they decide to marry on their own. Many working women feel there would be greater understanding in love

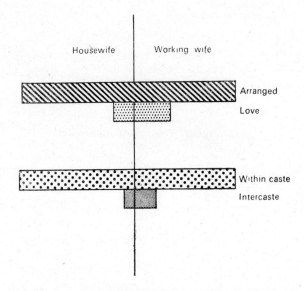

Fig. 3. Type of marriage in relation to occupational status.

marriages and fewer objections to their working. It is also likely that working women marry late. Hence they go in for love marriage, as opposed to a conventional arranged marriage at an earlier age. Working women favour their own choice of marriage partners. Only 62% of working women chose an arranged marriage against 86% of non-working housewives who prefer an arranged match.

The majority of Indian women are satisfied with their own type of marriage, but the ones who have had arranged marriages feel more secure. While 90% of those who had arranged marriages do not regret it, only 80% of those who married for love are happy about it afterwards. The diversity in habits and customs, language, food, and dress that prevails in India imposes greater strain on the couples who had love marriages than on those who had arranged marriages. This may be the reason why an arranged match gives greater security and confidence to a woman.

Marital Happiness and Adjustment in Relation to Type of Marriage
Happiness in marriage is important for both arranged or love

matches. However, marital unhappiness increases from 7% in arranged marriage to 12% in love matches as seen in Table 3. In the in-between category of fairly happy marriages, arranged matches score over love matches. However, definite conclusions could not be drawn because the two groups were incomparable in size.

Table 3

COMPARISON OF TYPES OF MARRIAGE

Married life	Arranged Marriage		Love Marriage	
	No.	%	No.	%
Unhappy	55	7.19	14	12.18
Fairly happy	198	25.96	25	21.74
Happy	511	66.85	76	66.08
Total	764	100.00	115	100.00

In love marriage there is usually greater expectation on both sides as each partner expects more understanding from the other. After the romantic courting is over, when the couple is faced with the practical problems of marriage, they feel disillusioned and consider marriage less happy. A love marriage usually creates a greater problem between the woman's family and the man's, because of a communication gap, especially if it is a mixed marriage with the woman and man speaking different languages, having different eating habits, and observing different customs. There is a greater feeling of alienation, especially for the girl, who has to be accepted into the boy's family. With this, new problems in marriage crop up.

Srilata, a Maharashtrian interior decorator who had a love marriage, had a series of problems with her Bengali in-laws which caused her unhappiness. Srilata said that even after 6 years of married life she was never fully accepted as a member of her in-law's household. Her husband was unhappy with her because she had not made a serious effort to learn Bengali. Living in Bombay it was difficult for her to learn the language. Srilata was convinced that much greater effort was needed on the part of both the husband and wife to make a love marriage a success than was required in an arranged marriage.

Sushma spoke of her experience. "I had a love marriage and I am very happy. Because I loved my husband and married, I have not neglected any of my obligations to him, our children, or his family. Whether a person makes a success of marriage or not depends more on the individual than on the type of marriage."

Love marriages, however, create certain specific adjustment problems almost from the very beginning. Over 15% of such marriages have adjustment problems against only 8% in arranged marriages. In India, when a girl marries, she gets wedded to a family as well and this leads to additional problems.

Mrs Sampath, who had a love marriage within her own caste, narrated her problems. "My in-laws thought I had grabbed their son. They insulted me and my family. In addition, overnight, they expected me to become very fond of them. For their part, they showed no sympathy or love towards me. My husband also expected me to abide by the wishes of his parents. It took us months to understand one another's point of view."

Chandrika Soni, after a love marriage, had initial adjustment problems, but feels she enjoys a happy life. As she was a Malayali and her husband a Dogra, she felt out of place in her in-law's place. Since she could not speak a word of Hindi, she had real difficulty in communicating with her in-laws. She was treated like a novelty piece in their home. She says, "Luckily for me, I did not stay with my in-laws always. We visited them only occasionally and stayed with them during holidays. But my husband expected me to undergo a full transformation in my tastes and habits which was very difficult for me to accept. With time, we both realised that there is a lot of adjustment needed to make a happy marriage. Being married to a Dogra, I have also changed, and I am sure living with a Malayali has changed my husband too."

Girls who go in for love marriage are usually more independent and self-willed. They are likely to be less adjusting than girls who go through a conventionally arranged wedding. Usually love marriages cross barriers of caste and class and these add certain specific problems to marital adjustments. Girls having an arranged match are probably mentally prepared and go through the initial adjustment to marriage more easily.

In nearly 67% cases the Indian woman makes a success of her marriage, whether it is love or arranged. She is family-bound and her domestic ties are strong. Whatever the type of marriage, their intention is to make a happy home and have a happy married life together. It is interesting to note that whatever the type of marriage, about 20% of the women fit into the fairly happy/unhappy marriage. These women, having no definite convictions, sail through life tackling problems but consider themselves fairly happy in spite of the external circumstances.

Inter-caste Marriage

As previously mentioned, most Indian marriages are caste endogamous. Though marriages occasionally do occur between a man and woman of different *jatis* the vast majority of marriages take place within the prescribed caste restrictions and conventions. In the present study, over 90% of the marriages are caste endogamous. Modern India, however, has seen a breaking away from caste restrictions. This has, to some extent, affected the marriage pattern in the country. In the urban educated population inter-caste marriages do occur occasionally and are being accepted by society.

Though legally inter-caste marriages are given full recognition, a conservative society accepts them less readily. Besides, in a vast multilingual country like ours, there is a communication gap between different castes speaking the same language and the same castes speaking different languages. Education alone can remove the compartmentalisation of caste practices and give a wider understanding of the homogeneity of Indian society.

Occupational Status and Inter-caste Marriage

With the increase in women's education and the independence that comes from employment, inter-caste marriages are increasing in number. Though only about 8% of housewives had inter-caste marriages, the percentage moved up to over 20% in the working women's group (Fig. 3).

The working woman is less influenced by authority and tradition and is psychologically more prepared than a typical housewife to enter into an unconventional marriage partnership. The working woman has greater opportunity to select her life partner on her own as she is likely to have greater exposure to men at the place of work. Though over 75% of working women have had conventional caste marriages, they are definitely more progressive and less biased about inter-caste marriages than housewives.

A difference of caste definitely adds certain risks to marriage. More adjustment and understanding will be needed to make an inter-caste marriage a success. A working woman is willing to take this risk. If for some reason the marriage fails, she can take care of herself without depending on her family. Women who have never contemplated employment are less likely to go in for inter-caste marriages. Families very rarely arrange an inter-caste marriage. Marriages outside the caste are usually love marriages. Hence it is not surprising that more working women end up with inter-caste marriages than non-working women.

Education and Inter-caste Marriage

Education and economic independence are the two main factors which help a woman to exercise her rights as an individual. Once a woman is economically self-sufficient, she has greater freedom to act of her own accord.

As seen in Fig. 4, the percentage of inter-caste marriage doubled in the college educated group and increased four times in the

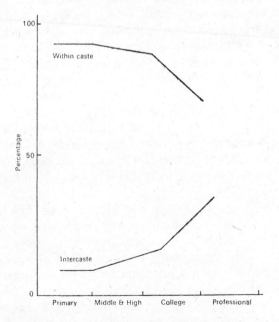

Fig. 4. Type of marriage according to educational level.

professional group. Along with increased education, women are likely to enjoy greater freedom and independence. Professional women, with their career contacts, exercise greater authority in the selection of a marriage partner for themselves. In spite of all these differences, we find that about 90% of women have caste marriages which shows how traditional our society is.

PROFILE FOR AN ELIGIBLE MARRIAGE PARTNER

Though the great majority of Indian women agree to an arranged marriage within their caste what do they value most in their husband? Success in marriage is partly a matter of finding the right person and partly of being the right person. Some of the important personality characteristics that go to make a right person in the views of women are revealed in this study. Irrespective of the area of origin and education, the respondents in this study prefer husbands of good character which they feel is the most important consideration. If the man is essentially good, the path to better adjustment in marriage is clear. Women of the upper and middle socio-economic strata ranked superior intelligence second, having a good position and status third, family background fourth, and physical charm last. Women of the lower strata, however, from all the areas gave fifth rank to intelligence. Position and earnings took precedence over intelligence for this group of women.

Among the poor, primary consideration is given to character and then to what a man can earn. Very often the main problem for the urban poor is that their men fall prey to the numerous temptations of city life and squander whatever money they make. Then the woman has to work to support herself and her children. The economic distress and squalor in which the urban poor live is aggravated in many cases by the man's neglect of his wife and family.

It is interesting to note that character is given first place by women of all levels of education, except professional women in the West and the North who consider intelligence above character. The Indian woman, being fairly tradition-bound and conservative, wants to be sure of a man's character before any other factor is considered. Her excessive concern about goodness in the male is not only due to the fact that in her upbringing she has repeatedly heard that character is what she should look for in the male, but because of her psychological make-up she needs emotional security. She wants to be sure that her husband will be a man who will truthfully abide by the obligations and responsibilities of a marriage.

Intelligence and education take second rank especially among the educated and the upper socio-economic group. The better placed in society know the importance of education and intelligence and they feel certain a person who has these will automatically do well in life. Women in this group would like to have husbands better educated than themselves. This is a social pattern so sharply defined that to deviate from this would be considered as risking the chances of success in marriage. In India we find a lot of difference in the educational level of the husband and wife leading to a lack of companionship, but more often the wife is unaware of such a lack and complacently devotes herself to the needs of the husband and children.

Although the background ranks low in the priorities, it is considered important in the total evaluation of a desirable partner. Usually in most arranged marriages, eligibility is synonymous with a good family background. Since the individual characteristics dominate over the environmental characteristics for a marriage partnership, the respondents must have ranked the former above the latter.

Besides, in an urban population the idea of background becomes less significant. The families are smaller, more mobile and often away from the place of origin. Young men may be away from home either for higher studies or work and it becomes difficult to know the full background of a person. In such cases individual merit is considered more important than other factors. Looks too are rated low. This is probably a part of the socialization process. This probably makes her say instinctively that a man's character is of greater worth than his looks.

FACTORS RELATING TO MARITAL HAPPINESS AND ADJUSTMENT

Questions regarding marital happiness are asked over and over again. When a man and woman from different backgrounds marry, a lot of adjustments have to be made. We have considered the different characteristics one would look for in a male as a marriage partner. Let us now consider some of the factors which make the right partners for marriage. First of all let us see the situational characteristics in relation to marital happiness and adjustment.

Situational Characteristics

The situational characteristics for a woman include her socio-economic status, educational level, parent's married life, type of family, size of family, ordinal position etc.

Socio-economic Status

Marital adjustment becomes easier when the socio-economic status of a family improves. In the lowest group only about half of them reported easy adjustment, while in the middle strata over 65% and in the upper strata 75% were happily adjusted in marriage. With economic development social status also improves, and woman enjoy greater freedom and equality. Only in the case of the northern zone does one find the percentage of easy marital adjustment the same in all three stratas. In other areas, the marital adjustment score is significantly less for the lowest socio-economic group.

In the North, it is observed that even in the lowest strata, men do not allow women to go out for menial jobs as they consider it below their dignity. Even if the family is impoverished, women

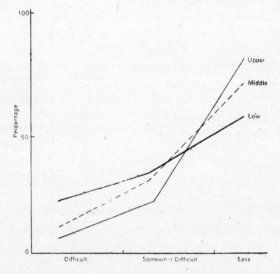

Fig. 5. Marital adjustment in relation to socio-economic status.

usually do not go out of their homes to do menial work. This probably elevates a woman's status in the home. She is able to play her role as a wife more effectively, and gain her husband's love and confidence. Besides, the overall economic level of the Northern states is much better than that of the rest of India. The better economic level of the North, even of the lowest lot, relieves domestic tension and makes adjustment easier for men and women (Table 4 and Fig. 5). The same material affluence must be responsible for reducing the proportion of women who adjust easily to marriage in the higher strata. Material affluence reduces individual aspirations for women, resulting in boredom and frustration which eventually create temperamental conflict between the spouses.

Education

What relationship does marital happiness have with education? Parents often say, "Girls should not be educated as highly as boys because the more knowledgeable they are the less they are likely to submit to any external control." Even if they respect their husbands or the heads of their families, they may not willingly accept authority if they are given liberal opportunities of learning. They would be less prone to blindly accept the behaviour pattern of their husbands, as is traditional. When their is no opposition of ideas, there is less chance of interactional problems. But on the other hand, if husband and wife are open-minded and accept each other's ideas objectively, there is a better chance of leading a fuller and happier life even with a high level of education.

The present study shows that in all socio-economic strata, higher education for girls results in better adjustment in marriages, except in the minority group of professional women whose marital adjustment is more difficult than in the case of college educated women. This might be due to their profession which creates conflict between their familial and career roles. That is why some of these women said those who choose a career should not get married, so that they can concentrate on the job rather than being dissatisfied on both fronts.

Some women who are gainfully employed outside their homes try to make up for their absence by devoting full attention to the home when they return. They try to give an impression to others that they are managing both fronts efficiently. This is very difficult to keep up for a long time. When a woman takes up outside em-

Table 4

MARITAL ADJUSTMENT ACCORDING TO SOCIO-ECONOMIC STATUS IN DIFFERENT REGIONS

Responses	East		West		South		North		Central		Total	
	No.	%	No.	%	No.	%	No.	%	No.	%	No.	%
Upper												
Difficult	2	4.76	1	2.08	1	2.32	2	5.55	3	7.14	9	4.24
Somewhat difficult	8	19.05	10	20.81	10	23.25	11	30.55	1	2.38	40	18.86
Easy	32	76.18	38	77.11	32	74.43	23	63.90	38	90.48	163	76.90
Middle												
Difficult	12	14.12	6	6.81	4	4.82	4	4.49	5	5.68	31	7.16
Somewhat difficult	20	23.53	22	25.01	25	30.12	25	28.01	16	18.18	108	24.94
Easy	53	62.35	60	68.18	54	65.06	60	67.50	67	76.14	294	67.90
Low												
Difficult	11	22.93	7	15.90	10	21.29	7	14.58	8	17.39	43	18.55
Somewhat difficult	9	18.74	16	36.36	18	38.29	8	16.67	12	26.08	63	27.04
Easy	28	58.33	21	47.74	19	40.42	33	68.75	26	56.53	127	54.41
Total												
Difficult	25	14.29	14	7.73	15	9.20	13	7.51	16	9.09	83	9.45
Somewhat difficult	37	21.14	48	26.51	53	26.40	44	25.43	29	16.47	211	24.03
Easy	113	64.57	119	65.76	105	64.40	116	67.06	131	74.44	584	66.52
	175	100.00	181	100.00	173	100.00	173	100.00	176	100.00	878	100.00

ployment, some sacrifices have to be made in the home. The expectation by each family member also has to be reduced. Only adjustments make married life happy.

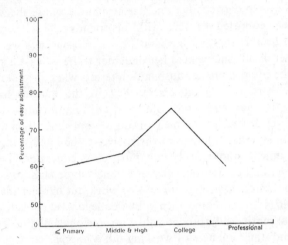

Fig. 6. Marital adjustment according to educational level.

Maya Rao, who was a senior executive in the L.I.C. before marriage, openly admitted that she had no interest in household affairs. She said, "My husband thinks he has succeeded in changing my mind and I have happily accepted the domestic role. But he is mistaken. My primary unhappiness in marriage is that I cannot mentally reconcile myself to a purely domestic role." Mrs Devraj, a professionally qualified nurse, also felt the same way. "My husband does not mind my qualification, but he does not approve of my working. I can never accept my marriage happily unless I am allowed to work and use my knowledge."

The more educated a women is, especially after a certain level of education, the more complicated her married life becomes. She becomes less compromising, more independent in her views, and more preocccupied with intellectual pursuits. This causes frustration in her married life.

Women who are not educated or those who have minimal education have their own specific problems which cause marital unhappiness in less than 20% of the cases reviewed. There is a great communication gap between the husband and wife if the husband is educated and the wife is not. They have less to share as the husband and wife frequently live and move in spheres of their own.

Premlata Shetty had only passed middle school. She felt there was a great gap between her and her husband because she was not sufficiently educated to mix with his friends and colleagues. She admitted frankly that her husband's work and business were much above her head. She wanted her daughter to be at least a graduate so that she could share her husband's interests when she got married.

When there is a great discrepancy in the educational status between the husband and wife, marital relationships becomes strained. Educated young men of today want more than domestic caretakers as wives. They want their wives to be intelligent, smart, and be able to move easily in company. As education gives more knowledge, builds up taste, increases one's understanding, women who are better educated are able to work out happier marriages. Our findings reveal that women with a college level education have the easiest marital adjustment unlike professionals or the less educated, and their chances of working out a happy marriage are the highest percentage (see Fig. 6). This definitely shows that the educational level of a woman is a very important factor in marital happiness and adjustment to marriage itself.

Type of Family

What is the relationship between marital adjustment and type of family? Table 5 shows that marital adjustment is almost the same whether the family is nuclear or joint. The nuclear family makes adjustment slightly easier because the wife faces less interference from in-laws. The wife has greater freedom to function on her own. She has greater privacy with her husband and gets to know her husband quicker. As the husband's parents are not staying in the same house, the wife does not have to tackle the generation gap. When the girl does not enter into a joint family, she is able to continue the life she was used to before marriage. There is no need for any major adjustments.

Even little things bother a girl entering a joint family if she is not used to it. From childhood Sulekha was used to bathing in warm water. When she entered her husband's joint family she had to bathe in cold water as no one in her husband's house believed in having hot water baths. When she expressed her wish to have a hot bath, everyone made fun of her as if she was wanting something most un-usual. In another case, Leela had to stop wearing two braids as her in-laws did not approve of it. In most instances in spite of these initial minor adjustment problems, marital life goes on smoothly.

Table 5

MARITAL ADJUSTMENT IN RELATION TO TYPE OF FAMILY

Marital Adjustment	Nuclear Family		Joint Family	
	No.	%	No.	%
Difficult	51	9.40	32	9.52
Somewhat difficult	114	21.03	97	28.87
Easy	377	69.57	207	61.61
Total	542	100.00	336	100.00

For a bride to fit into a joint family poses innumerable problems, especially if the husband's family is very traditional. In some cases, the girl has to suppress her personality and undergo an almost complete transformation.

Usha was educated in a public school in Simla. After her schooling she went to college in Bombay staying with her parents and two brothers. Marriage brought about a big change. She had to move to Kanpur to live with her in-laws as her husband was in his family business. From a family of five members she had to move into a household of over 20 people. She felt she had lost her freedom, privacy and comfort. Though she and her husband had a bedroom, it was as a passage-cum-living room used by all. The couple did not have any privacy in the house nor could she have a word with her husband without someone overhearing it. Usha was almost a mental wreck for the first year of her marriage. She did not have the courage to tell her parents about her problems and make them un-happy. Time the great healer gradually brought about a change in her. She willed herself to accept community living without com-plaining.

She is now of the opinion that "one must have a great capacity to give and share, listen and obey, if one wants to make a happy life in a joint family. Maybe I, being the eldest among three children and the only daughter, was used to having more freedom and was over-pampered in my house. Probably this was the reason why I took time to adjust after marriage in my new home."

One tends to think that the ordinal position does have some bearing on the moulding of one's personality. With different ordinal positions, the personal social environment of individuals differ and hence one can turn out to be assertive and aggressive, according to that particular environment, or can become docile and submissive in a different environment where one has to listen to everyone. Studies have revealed the desirability of the middle-borns, who are capable of give and take, towards actually promoting marital happiness. But this need not be the case. One cannot choose one's ordinal position, but the environment created affects the development of the child in making her an accommodating individual.

The present study did not reveal any relationship between a woman's ordinal position and her marital adjustment (see Table 6). Approximately two-thirds of those interviewed were happy and made easy adjustments regardless of their ordinal positions. There was hardly any difference between the first born, middle born and the youngest.

Table 6

MARITAL ADJUSTMENT OF WOMEN ACCORDING TO ORDINAL POSITION

Marital adjustment	First born		In between		Last		Only child	
	No.	%	No.	%	No.	%	No.	%
Difficult	27	10.22	41	8.91	13	10.49	2	6.67
Somewhat difficult	51	19.31	121	26.34	28	22.58	11	36.67
Easy	186	70.47	298	64.75	83	66.93	17	56.66
Total	264	100.00	460	100.00	124	100.00	30	100.00

The difference was mainly seen in case of an only child who, having grown up alone is more demanding, less compromising and therefore less prone to making adjustments.

Pankajam Srinivasan and Vimla Tiwari were the only children in their respective families. Their stories are very similar. Pankajam, after marriage, moved to Madras to live with her husband, his parents, two sisters and a brother. Her sisters-in-law and brother-in-law were all studying in college. Her father-in-law was an invalid and her mother-in-law was preoccupied with fasts and pujas. The husband left early in the morning and got back very late at night. Pankajam felt she was not given any love or recognition by anyone in the family. She had to work the whole day, attending to everyone's comfort, while no one bothered about her. This feeling of frustration affected her relationship with her husband and made her marriage unhappy.

Mrs Tiwari too had a lot of problems with her husband and his family as she felt that she was never respected by anyone, not even by the servants. She was sure her mother-in-law was more affectionate to the two younger daughters-in-law than to her, and this feeling of inferiority marred her marital happiness.

Mrs Reddy, also an only child, spoke highly of her loving husband and said, "My husband knows I am a pampered daughter. Hence he is very careful never to hurt my feelings. Sometime back when my mother-in-law and father-in-law came to stay with us, my husband openly told them that I am very sensitive and hence they must treat me like another daughter in the family and not as a daughter-in-law. Everyone in the family understands this and treats me with great affection. Because of the warmth and understanding shown by my husband and his family I had no problem adjusting to marriage."

Size of Family of Orientation

It is generally felt that large families create an environment of give and take and individuals who grow up in that kind of environment seldom become self-centered. In this study it was seen that regarding marital happiness, there was only a marginal difference between girls coming from small, medium, and large families. On the whole over 60% made a fairly easy adjustment regardless of the size of their parental families. There are other intervening variables more powerful than family size and ordinal position which cause marital unhappiness.

In the present study, however, it was found that girls coming from medium sized families tend to have less problems of adjustment. Some girls from large families are especially lost and unhappy when they have to live alone with their husbands in far off places. Mrs Bhava, one of 11 children, had to move to Hyderabad with her husband after marriage. For months she could not adjust to her new life alone with a man. She used to get fits of crying thinking of her home, which she could never explain to her husband. Her husband would get very annoyed with her and this seriously hampered marital adjustment.

Some girls from large families develop an inferiority complex due to neglect and heavy domestic responsibilities. Mrs Neeraja was the eldest of eight. She had to bear the entire responsibility of the kitchen and take care of her brothers and sisters as her mother was pregnant most of the time or had just had a baby. She always felt that there was no one who really cared for her while she herself was always attending to other's needs. Even after marriage she found it was the same. She had to please her in-laws and husband, with the result a sense of neglect and inferiority coloured her entire life affecting marital adjustment. Too many responsibilities also prove a strain on marital adjustment and marital happiness.

Parents' Married Life

Heredity and environment both affect children's development. The social environment of the parents has an impact on the personality development of children. A maladjusted marriage is likely to affect the child adversely. If the girl grows up by rebelling, the same reflex is likely to operate in the interaction between her spouse and herself. This will obviously create marital maladjustment.

Childhood security is a major factor that decides the entire personality of an individual. If the parents have marital problems, their children become unstable and insecure. This leads to a negative attitude to marriage in adulthood because of the unhappiness one has seen in the lives of one's parents. In our study we came across girls hating the idea of marriage after having seen their parents' married life.

Table 7

MARRIED LIFE OF PARENTS AND THE RESPONDENTS' MARRIED LIFE

| | Parents' married life | | | |
	Unhappy	Fairly happy	Happy	Total
Married life				
Unhappy	10	28	31	69
Fairly happy	10	77	136	223
Happy	7	81	499	587
Total	27	186	666	879

The X^2 value computed between the parents' married life and the respondents' married life is 103.75, which is highly significant.

There was abundant evidence of this even in our survey. Each individual constitutes a pattern of hereditary potentialities developed to a greater or lesser extent under the impact of various environmental influences. Environment, if improved, will have a marked effect on the individual. When we were dealing with selected characteristics in a marriage partner, many considered family background important. This is especially so in arranged marriages. The maturity of the individual is assessed according to the stability of the family background.

Parents emphasize this point a great deal in selecting marriage partners for their children, whereas in love marriages only the individual concerned is thought to be important, which is an imperfect perspective for marriage in the Indian context.

Lata Sekhar's earliest impression of her parents was that of an

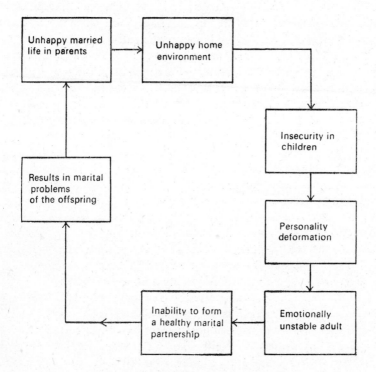

Fig. 7. Effect of parental discord on daughter.

exchange of blows. On her part this lead to a great dread of marriage in adolescence. Somehow she got acquainted with a boy, got married in spite of her negative approach. After marriage she had numerous problems for which she blamed her husband. A deeper study made it obvious that she had no knowledge of how to adjust, hence her rigidity and destructive attitude were mainly responsible for her marital maladjustment. Her warped personality prevented her from establishing a healthy marital relationship. Meenakshi's case was one such. Meenakshi's mother was a frustrated person. She continuously misguided her daughter and complicated the latter's married life. Women coming from unhappy homes inevitably fail to work out a happy marriage.

Occupational Status

Does adjustment in marriage become difficult when the woman works? The working woman is not a new phenomenon. A rural culture which is predominantly agricultural does not impose any major adjustment problems in marriage even when the woman plays a vital role outside the home, participating with the male in sowing, planting, husking and pounding. In the urban sphere women have also been working for a long time in factories as menials and labourers. With better education women have entered every sphere of employment. Often they compete with men for jobs. These jobs consume a major slice of their time and leisure. Balancing domesticity with a career imposes a serious strain on the woman, more so if there are growing children and undue responsibilities. In the process marital harmony has often to be sacrificed and marital happiness is jeopardised.

Padmini's case is an instance in point. Though her husband had no objection to her working, he expected her to be a perfect house-wife. As they could not afford a full-time servant, she had to undertake a considerable portion of the daily chores. The meals had to be good, she had to keep her husband's things in order, do the marketing, the pressing and sewing, and an endless series of predictable and unpredictable duties. The daily wear and tear soon began to tell and irritability and exhaustion marred marital bliss. Perceptibly a working wife almost always has greater difficulty in adjusting to marriage. While over 70% housewives made easy marital adjustments, only a little over 50% of working wives claimed easy adjustment (Fig. 8). For women, family obligations are deemed primary, while the career is to be integrated into this general pattern and is allowed secondary interest at the most. If a woman happens to derive primary satisfaction from her career, she might experience conflict in her family relationship and find it difficult to integrate the interests of career and family.

Nowadays many qualified women want to combine the two rather than give up one for the other. A woman's position in and outside the home is so closely linked that it is very difficult to separate the two. Hence these women have almost insurmountable problems

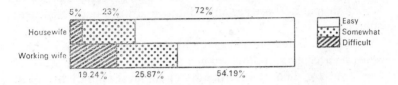

Fig. 8. *Marital adjustment in relation to occupational status.*

especially in the early years of marriage. Mrs Basu finds her dual role extremely difficult. "My in-laws accuse me of neglecting my home because I work in a school. They want me to give up my job. My husband also feels there is no need for me to work since he earns enough. I enjoy my work and continue working against everyone wishes. This is a cause of constant mental and physical strain to me."

Jayashri's case was more interesting in that imaginary anxieties stood in the way of a smooth adjustment. Jayashri's husband, in the early stages of marriage, was suspicious of the freedom she enjoyed as a working woman. She had no problem managing the home as there were only the two of them and she had a reliable servant. The main problem was her husband's suspicions. He thought her job as secretary may involve promiscuity. If she came home late from office he would ask her innumerable questions, and Jayashri would be annoyed.

Some working women become bossy and authoritative because they earn as much as their husbands do. Mrs Chari, running her father's confectionary store, asserted that every woman had the right to be whatever she chose. "Just because I am married I cannot become my husband's property. My husband works at Bhopal, but I have decided to establish my business here. I have openly told my husband that I cannot run around him and sacrifice my other interests."

A non-working housewife is willing to play her traditional role as a wife and mother. There are no conflicting demands which clash with her married life. She easily accepts man as the one wielding power and authority and plays a subservient role to him.

Marriage, like any other vocation in life, demands devotion, time, and energy if it is to prosper. If both husband and wife are lost in their individual ambitions and achievements, the house and family are bound to suffer. Adjustment to marriages becomes difficult unless both partners are accommodating and work out a convenient solution.

Mrs Nath, a doctor, said that a husband has numerous problems when he accepts a working woman as his wife, someone who has less time for him and the family. "I am most appreciative of my husband. He has stood by me through all the years of my career. He has had to sacrifice many of his personal interests because of the extra time he gives to the family and home."

INTERACTIONAL PATTERN

The interactional pattern of a couple may or may not click and can accordingly cause marital happiness or discord. Life styles and the interactional pattern in the family would include task differentiation, equal participation in family matters, an understanding husband, the husband discussing professional problems with his wife, the wife seeking advice from husband and elders, abiding by the husband's wishes, his attitude towards the wife's relatives, and many other aspects. Let us consider a few of them.

Task Differentiation

The management of the traditional joint family is primarily the wife's duty. She runs the household and helps the husband by contributing her labour as much as possible. Although both husband and wife have to make adjustments, wives adjust more than husbands. Wives fit more easily into the institutional requirements of marriage, in that the home and children are more nearly the centre of their lives.

Today's married couples, especially in nuclear families, are learning the meaning of shared home-making. Both men and women find companionship and mutual understanding in this new pattern of partnership. A significant change in the division of labour within the family is apparent among the urban middle-class. More women are going out to work. They earn part of the family income. They participate in making decisions for the family. The husbands share some of the household chores with the wife. In almost all activities the wife's autonomy prevails except in the case of financial management when the differentiation pattern submits to the husband's autonomy. In other activities syncratic co-operation is very evident.

The husband's help in domestic chores is a contributing factor in marital happiness. By working together, the couple find not only love but also comradeship and delight in each other. Thus they build all dimensions of family life together. In this survey it was seen that among women who get help from their husbands over 85% are very happy in marriage.

But it is also true that over 40% who do not get any help are also happy. Usually housewives do not expect any help from the husband in domestic duties. Besides, in India we can hire help at a reasonable rate and thus relieve the housewife of a lot of domestic work. The problem really arises when the wife is gainfully employed and has no domestic aid. Then she expects her husband's help.

In the middle socio-economic strata the wife often expects the husband's help in marketing, taking the children to school, helping in their studies, fetching the morning milk, giving her a hand in cleaning the house when there is extra work, or occasionally even going into the kitchen when she is ill or has heavier work than she can manage. She does not expect nor would like her husband to step in and do a woman's job. She is happier when he shoulders the family responsibilities of providing and protecting.

The majority of Indian men are not indifferent to their wives' problems. About 30% of them are unable to help them in household responsibilities, due to their own preoccupation with work. The division of labour is conveniently accepted by the average male and female. Man takes care of outside work and woman the domestic front.

Surjeeth Kaur, a simple Punjabi woman, wife of a car mechanic, had this to say: "Our home is a happy home because we respect each other. I do not think there is anything my husband will refuse to do. But I would hate to see Sardar Sahib do a woman's job.

Does he expect me to sit in his shop and repair the cars like a man? He gives me whatever money I need to run our home. Why should I bother him about other things in the house?"

In other instances, we see the rigid division of labour between husband and wife in nuclear family set-ups. The slightest deviation causes friction. This again is not satisfactory in a family situation. Once a man and woman have developed mutual respect for each other, it matters little who does what or how much. What a woman usually expects from her husband is that he should be understanding and considerate especially when she is overburdened with domestic chores.

Adjustment to marriage definitely becomes easier if the husband's help is available, even if occasional. But a husband's help with domestic chores is not obligatory for easy marital adjustment. What most women, including those of the lower strata, disapprove of is the indifference of some men to women's tasks.

Mrs Srilakshmi aptly explained this. "I do not want my husband to do all my work in the kitchen but what has always stood in the way of my adjusting to marriage happily is his unconcern. Even if I am ill, or there is an extra load of work, he thinks it is my headache. This has always made me angry. Even my maid-servant is luckier. When she is late in going home from work, her husband does part of the evening cooking. Consideration is an inherent part of one's character. I am simply unfortunate in having a selfish husband. All that matters to him is his work, his comfort, and his relaxation."

Mrs Sridhar, a full-time lecturer in a college, felt strongly that in today's world man is not the only bread-earner and woman is not the sole caretaker of the home and of domestic duties. When the woman contributes her earnings to the home and family, man has to share the household work and lessen the woman's burden. Mrs Sridhar has a nuclear family with three school-going children. The husband takes the children to school and brings them back at lunch time and sees to it that they have lunch and then returns to his office. She usually gets home in the evening by 4.30 p.m. Often her husband gives her a hand in the kitchen also. Morning tea is always his duty. While she fixes the breakfast, the husband prepares the children for school.

True, working and combining the responsibilities of a home become very difficult if the husband gives no help at all . In Mrs

Sridhar's case adjustment to marriage was easy in spite of her being a full-time lecturer, because of the help and co-operation she received from her husband from the beginning.

The women interviewed gave numerous examples of their husbands participation in household activities. Mrs Nair, wife of a company executive, said, "My husband always does the Sunday marketing." Mrs Kulkarni, a teacher, is greateful to her husband who helps in various household duties. He shampoos the children at weekends, helps with the ironing of clothes, defreezes the refrigerator, and takes the children on outings to give her a little respite. Mrs Lakshmi mentioned that her husband always takes over kitchen duties when she is ill or during her menstruation. Many more women from nuclear families spoke of their husband's contribution to lighten the domestic load.

The Indian male is not as concerned about keeping his wife happy as she is about his personal comforts and needs. In small families the husband frequently makes his contribution to case the wife's domestic responsibilities. We find about 17% of them always helping with household chores and 53% sometimes, and when the need arises.

Understanding Nature of the Husband

Many women mentioned that the understanding and friendliness which the husbands had shown after marriage made adjustment to marriage easy and pleasant. As shown in Fig. 9, nearly 86% had easy marital adjustment where husbands are always understanding. If the husbands are not understanding, 60% of women found it difficult to adjust to marriage. In spite of the understanding nature of the husband, about 17% wives do not adjust easily to marriage.

It takes the right man and the right woman to make marriage a success. It is not enough for the man alone to be understanding or the woman alone to be kind and sympathetic. In this study, some of the respondents remembered vividly instances when husbands were kind to them. Mrs Kantikar recollected how much she dreaded getting married and moving away to the new city. Her marriage was a typically arranged one. To her pleasant surprise, within a couple of days she knew she had a friend in her husband. He was mature, protecting, and affectionate. She has now been married over 12 years and said she has had no major problems.

Savitri Sanyal's case was slightly different, but even in her case the husband's positive role helped to make an easier adjustment. Savitri moved to Calcutta from the Malda district after marriage to live with her husband who was a tailor. She was terribly shy and nervous and dreaded sleeping with a man. Her husband was so understanding that he never compelled her to go to bed with him till she wanted it. It took nearly three months to get over her fear. All through this time her husband was extremely patient and never forced himself on her.

Numerous instance were mentioned where the husband and even the in-laws helped the new bride to adjust to her life as a married woman. Poonam Uppal was just 19 when she got married. Shyly she admitted, "I did not even know how to make 'phulkas'. I clearly remember the first few months of our marriage. My husband used to cook the evening meal and teach me cooking. As he had lived as a bachelor away from his parents he knew cooking."

When a husband tells his wife about his salary or income, promotions, likely change of job or transfer, difficulties with his boss or colleagues, the wife gains greater confidence. Her bond with her husband gets stronger.

For instance, in cases where the husband never discusses his work, the wife feels she is completely excluded from a major part of his life. She even feels insecure sometimes not knowing her husband's full assets and liabilities. In small nuclear families, the husband and wife bond becomes much stronger when the husband frankly discusses with his wife his work and his problems.

The average woman probably knows little about the outside world. She can, however, give confidence and inspire her husband to work better if there is good communication, which can create the atmosphere for optimum family development.

Mrs Panigrahi lamented, "There is a barrier between my husband and myself. From the very beginning of my married life I knew there were certain things my husband never discussed with me. Even now I do not know how much he earns, how much he gives away to his mother or how much he puts aside for me and the children. Though I am a science graduate, my husband feels a woman should confine her interests to the home and children and should not interfere in her husband's work."

Hera Devi, though only a barber's wife, proudly said that whatever her husband earned he brought home. He always told her how much he made and what he had done throughout the day. When

the husband does not discuss his professional problems with the
wife, 80% wives become unhappy in marriage. When the husband
freely discusses his work and problems with the wife, the percentage
of unhappy wives is only 34%. But even when the husband does

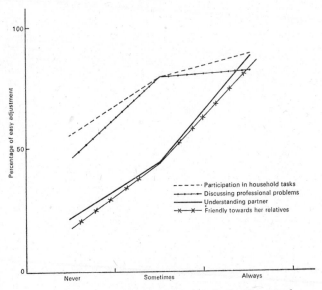

*Fig. 9. Marital adjustment in relation to husband's attitude
and role participation.*

not share his professional problems with his wife, over 50% are
happy in marriage. This shows that the husband's sharing of professional problems with his better half is not a deciding factor in
marital happiness. The average female does not seriously bother
when the husband does not confide in her about his work, as even
among the happily married only 14% of husbands discuss their
work problems with their wives. Only in certain cases is the husband
willing to discuss his professional problems with his wife effectively. If the woman is illiterate and ill experienced, the husband
talking about his problems will only aggravate the woman's
worries. A rich, illiterate woman married to a businees man is not
the least bit bothered about how the money comes for her sarees
and jewellery, or what her husband does to amass a fortune. All
that she is interested in is that her husband should provide for her
needs. Some women mentioned that their husbands opened up
only if asked, about office or work problems. When they were

not asked, they chose to remain silent on matters pertaining to their professional work. This indicates that the male is not fond of discussing work and work problems unless compelled to. In a partriarchial society where woman has played a subservient role for thousands of years, this attitude is not surprising.

Mrs Nalini Khare, educated but a full-time housewife, wondered why a man had to discuss his professional problems and office worries with his wife when she cannot be of any help in these matters. "I do not bother my husband about the problems I have with cooking or running the houshold. It is my headache. I would drive him nuts if I did. The same applies to his problems at work. I would hate to worry about things which only he can handle."

But this attitude has changed considerably in recent years. A woman is no longer content with domestic chores alone, functioning mechanically as the caretaker of the house. Many of them, especially those who are educated, want to be involved with their husband's problems. The percentage is higher in the educated and professionally qualified women (Table 8).

Table 8

WOMAN'S PARTICIPATION IN DISCUSSING HUSBAND'S PROFESSIONAL PROBLEMS IN RELATION TO THE EDUCATIONAL LEVEL OF THE WIFE

Discussing professional problems	Illiterate & primary		Middle & high		College		Professional	
	No.	%	No.	%	No.	%	No.	%
Never	169	72.22	118	51.07	82	23.69	3	6.67
Sometimes	49	20.93	95	41.12	217	62.71	29	64.44
Often	16	6.85	18	7.81	47	13.60	13	28.89
Total	234	100.00	231	100.00	346	100.00	45	100.00

Happiness in a nuclear family grows with free exchange of ideas, shared values and the united tackling of problems. The intrests of husband and wife cannot be compartmentalised into separate units. The interests of one member of the family interacts on the interests of the other.

If a man marries an educated woman he should not exclude her from his activities. It is probably different in a male dominated social structure when a woman cannot even express the wish to share in her husband's professional or other interests. She accepts her specific role and expects nothing more.

Women's Role in Family Matters

To what extent does a woman contribute in decision making in family matters, and how does this affect her marital adjustment and happiness? In a traditional Indian home and more so if it is a joint family, the woman knows she cannot always have a say in family matters. The average woman knows many things would be beyond her understanding because of her inexperience in worldly matters. She is not frustrated because she cannot give her opinion on all family matters. Nearly 45% of the women questioned have

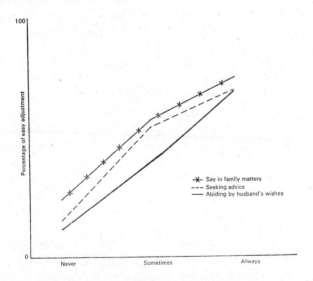

Fig. 10. Marital adjustment in relation to wife's attitude and role participational.

made easy marital adjustments even though they seldom have a say in family matters. When they have no role at all, the percentage of women who have made easy adjustment drops to 31% (Fig. 10).

Though a man may not take a woman into confidence about every family matter, she must surely be given a chance to speak for herself about matters concerning her life, their children, the rest of the family and home. This should be so even if she does

not make a contribution economically. When a woman is completely ignored and her husband acts independently, marital problems
arise. In certain cases, when the woman enjoys full freedom,
adjustment problems crop up because the woman becomes so
bossy at times that the man resents it. Some women who insist on
giving their opinion on all family matters may be the interfering,
nagging type who would make any marriage difficult.

In general then, when the woman has a say in family matters
the husband and wife work as a team taking each other into
confidence. The home is the main sphere of a typical housewife's
interest and activities. A marriage where the woman is given a
say in family matters is happier as the woman identifies herself
with the family. When she is discriminated against and excluded
from family affairs, she resents it. This resentment shows in her
attitude to home, husband, children and her entire marriage.

Attitude Towards Seeking Advice from Elders

Nearly 75% of women who always take the advice of others are
happy in marriage. While only 15% of women who do not take
such advice are happy. The ones who seek advice from others are
the adjustable type. They are usually more compromising and
willing to consider other people's opinions. Such a person will
more often take her husband's opinion in various matters. This
results in better understanding all round. A woman who seeks the
advice of her elders cannot be a headstrong person. She would be
willing to accept another's suggestion and advice about how to
make a happy marriage.

Mrs Puri, a film distributor's wife, said that before taking any
important step she always asked her husband and in-laws for their
opinions, as elders have more experience. One can surely use their
advice fruitfully. Mrs Puri felt the problem with young couples
today was that they think they know everything and certainly
more than others. This was often the cause of conflict in their
personal and married lives.

In India, elders often act as marriage counsellors. A girl who
seeks the advice of her elders is assured of their support in helping
her through difficult times. Mrs Patel is a happily married middle-
aged woman. She said she was always in the habit of seeking
advice even though ultimately she took decisions on her own.
When one acts independently one is likely to be selfish and

inconsiderate, she explained.

The great majority of Indian women seek the advice of elders. They are part of their families and their action and the action of others are closely interlinked. According to the cultural tradition in India, the wife consults her husband or her mother-in-law, the husband consults his father or elder brothers or uncle, the children their parents or grandparents and so it goes on. The elders are treated with respect and reverence in most Indian families. It matters very little who the elder is and whether the person is male or female. This attitude of seeking advice reveals the basic character of the Indian woman who is dependent, less educated than the male, and therefore relies on the opinion of others. She seeks advice, is willing to adjust and often abides by the advice of elders. This becomes a major contributing factor for marital happiness.

Willingness to Adjust

Marriage is smooth sailing when a woman is accommodating and abides by her husband's wishes. The average Indian wife, who is basically a family woman, would rather abide by her husband's wishes and find greater happiness in marriage than confront him and make her married life complicated and unhappy. Because of the woman's emotional, physical and economic dependence on the male, the man becomes more experienced and authoritative and the woman the helpmate and follower.

When a woman never abides by her husband and thinks and acts independently, in 62% of cases the marriage is unhappy. When a wife abides by her husband's wishes less than 5% are maritally unhappy. As in marital happiness, if a woman goes by her husband's wishes, adjustment to the rest of the changes that marriage entails is made easier. There is less confrontation between the male and female. Marriage, like any institution where co-operation and understanding are essential, cannot function smoothly if the partners are not willing to give in and abide by the other's wishes.

Mrs Sarojini Sinha, middle aged with a large bindi and saree covering her head said, "To whatever Sinha sahib says I listen, but ultimately he agrees to what I want. After all, any clever woman knows how to bring her husband round. By annoying a husband a woman can never get anything out of him. With love and persuasion she is sure to win him over."

Mrs Mythili Iyengar also expressed more or less the same view in different words. "True I always follow the wishes of my husband but I know my husband will never go against my wishes if I express them. We live in mutual trust and understanding, not by fighting a battle to prove whose wishes predominate."

In a traditional Indian marriage the woman is more compromising about the home and family. Man being the active bread earner and his role in sex also being more dominant, becomes more authoritative than the female. In a typical patriarchal society the male decides and the woman abides by his wishes.

The average woman would rather go by the wishes of the husband as long as he is not unreasonable. In most cases it becomes a mutual adjustment. Once the husband knows the wife is amicable and loving, he also gives in frequently to her wishes and helps to maintain the balance of the marriage partnership.

In the ultimate analysis of any situation in life, the quantum of happiness a woman or a man gets depends not on prestige and dominance, but on the feeling of security which comes from avoiding confrontation. A woman usually compromises on issues with her husband and is willing to subordinate her interests for the welfare of the home and married life. However, when it comes to matters of principle, she becomes the guiding force that inspires the husband. This is the basic strength of the Indian woman.

After marriage the girl leaves her parental home to become part and parcel of her new home with her husband and in-laws. In many instances it is she who maintains the stability and harmony of married life by her tolerance, willingness to adjust, compromise and sacrifice. After marriage, the Indian female undergoes a complete transformation in order to fit into her new role as wife. She is prepared to live with a new set of people, spend the rest of her life with her husband whose needs and desires she fulfils. She goes more by his wishes than her own. This typical trait of the Indian female has been developed by her playing a primary role in the welfare of the home and family for centuries. The husband, though the head of the family, generally creates a favourable environment to bring about a happy and healthy life after marriage.

Husband's Attitude towards Wife's Relatives

Married life can also be affected by the husband's attitude to his wife's relatives. The more cordial the husband's attitude, the more benign is the effect. Nearly 83% women are made happy by the husband's friendly attitude towards their family. Indian women are very attached to their parental families even after marriage. If the husband is the friendly type and gets on with her relatives, married life becomes happier. She gains confidence, feels that she is married to a friendly person. When the husband has shown a reverse attitude, 64% have resulted in unhappy marriages (Fig. 9).

More often than not Indian men are friendly towards their in-laws. Very often the fondness the husband shows for his wife's family is more than the wife's friendliness towards his family. This is because the son-in-law, whenever he visits his in-laws, is treated with great respect and love. There are less chances of confrontation between them. On the other hand, as the wife stays with his people, she has to face the usual mother-in-law/daughter-in-law problems which lead to conflict. Some women belonging to nuclear families, who have great control over their husbands, wean them away completely from their own families and make them get attached to the wives' parents, as illustrated in Jaya's case.

"My husband is more fond of my family than his own. He was so upset with his parents' behaviour towards my family, that we have not visited them for four years." Indira on the other hand said, "What difference does it make whether it is his parents or my parents. I treat his parents like my own and he has the greatest regard for mine. This has made the bond between us strong and close."

Mrs Vimla Swaroop narrated a different story. "My husband just dislikes my parents. He thinks they are not worth his respect because they are uncultured. If we quarrel he calls my father names and says I had no upbringing. He does not even approve of my visiting them during the children's holidays. In the early years of our marriage there was some misunderstanding between his parents and mine. My husband has carried on a grudge against them for over 10 years. This attitude has strained our marital relationship."

Mrs Srimati Srinivasan's marital problems were again centred around her husband's unfriendly attitude to her mother and eldest brother. The entire misunderstanding started over her wedding dowry. Her mother-in-law and husband felt the promised jewellery had not been given. Though married now for over five years the reproaches continue and Srimati is the poor victim.

Tara's case was very interesting. She came from a rich family in Rajasthan and was married to a doctor in Delhi. Her husband married her to please his parents. Within two weeks of marriage the husband decided Tara was not the girl for him. He began to make unreasonable demands on her parents. They tolerated this for some time. When they refused to oblige he made her life miserable. Tara has not thought of separation as she comes from a conservative family where no one even dreams of this.

For a girl her husband's friendly attitude to her people is a definite proof of his love for her. Very rarely will a wife disregard her family. So the husband's affection for her parents and relatives makes the marriage firm and contributes to its happiness.

MARITAL ADJUSTMENT PROBLEMS

The reasons for marital problems as expressed by the respondents were numerous. The predominant reasons were inadequate income, in-law problems and the difference in temperament between spouses.

Inadequate Income

In the low socio-economic strata, inadequate income is the prime cause for marital maladjustment. When people live a hand-to-mouth existence and the husband cannot provide for even the minimum necessities, marriage starts on a wrong note. The helpless wife either takes up employment to eke out a living or silently bears the unhappiness and misery marriage has brought her. In addition to not providing a square meal, if the husband is cruel and aggressive, the woman is miserable. In rare cases, she goes back to her parents or finds independent employment to support herself.

The abject poverty in which the urban poor live, lacking the basic necessities, colours their lives and causes great frustration in the male and female. This bears upon their marriage, family life and even work.

Malathi, a domestic servant, narrated her marital problems. "I have been married now for three years and live with my husband under the same roof but we hardly see each other. I work with my own hands to earn the money to support my daughter and myself. He has kept another woman on whom he spends all that he earns. I hope some day better sense will dawn on him."

When asked who manages her two year old child she said, "My neighbours are good. I give Rs 15 out of the Rs 70 I make to a neighbour who takes care of my child along with her own."

Thus marital adjustment becomes increasingly difficult in the lower socio-economic groups because of the great economic and

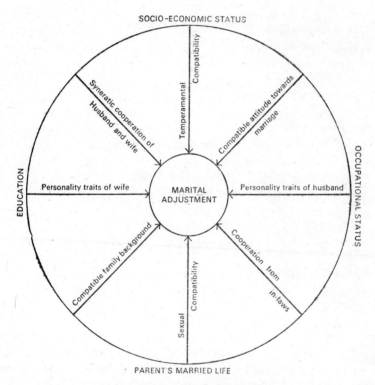

Fig. 10. Factors relating to marital adjustment.

psychological insecurity that exists among the urban poor. If a girl from the rural areas is married to someone in the city, she finds herself suddenly transported to a dirty, dingy, over crowded shack in the city. Unless her husband is able to compensate the material loss with his love, she is very soon disillusioned about the charms of marriage and of city life. If her husband has acquired the evils of city-life her hopes are shattered. She resents his drinking, gambling and squandering the meagre amount he earns on other women.

On the other hand, in higher socio-economic classes, adjustment to marriage becomes easier because women are less likely to be faced with the economic strain. There is greater intellectual and emotional compatibility between husband and wife. Women are treated with greater respect, more as companions and equals than as chattels to passively serve, slog, and suffer without complaining.

Difference in Temperament

It is interesting to note that both the low and high socio-economic groups gave the problems of difference in temperament as a reason for marital maladjustments. The cause too may be different but the outcome is the same.

In the lower socio-economic strata, when a couple is faced with inadequate financial resources to meet the daily requirements of life, dissatisfaction sets in. Both partners are bound to feel unhappy. Along with poverty, other social and psychological problems creep in. The low income group is usually faced with problems of ethics and morals. The husbands tend to be harsh on their wives as a re-action to the dissatisfaction with themselves.

If, however, the woman is clever and mentally strong, she works out a tangible solution. Sometimes she is able to persuade her man to shoulder the responsibilities of the home and family. Often she seeks employment to support herself and her children. Once she becomes too independent, she has no regard for the man, who often becomes a parasite, constantly demanding money.

Sometimes the harshness of the husband and in-laws begins with arguments about the dowry and other material benefits promised by the girl's parents. They are never satisfied with whatever they get and badger the girl. Take for instance Komal.

She had a conventional arranged marriage when she was 17. She being the only daughter, her parents lavished love and gifts on her which continued even after her marriage. Her husband and in-laws exploited the situation. They began to demand so much that it resulted in frequent misunderstandings between her husband and her parents. Then came a stage when Komal's husband wanted to invest all her jewellery and dowry in the family business. Her father, who had kept the money in her name, thought this was too unreasonable. When she went to meet her parents for a holiday, her father did not send her back. For over two years now she has been living with her parents and has no immediate plans for rejoining her husband. Her husband has written only once during the last two years. This also was a very formal letter to tell her that if she wanted to listen to her parents she need not return to him.

Mrs Swaroop faced serious problems with her husband because he was a typical society bird. He loved parties, late nights, and visiting people. She had been brought up in a very conservative environment by her father who was a strict disciplinarian. She did not temperamentally click with her husband. Her idea of a happy marriage was very different from what her actual marriage was and hence she has had bitter adjustment problems. She is now married for over 15 years and is fairly happy. Over the years she has learnt to be more communicative and sociable, and probably marriage and domestic responsiblities have sobered her husband also.

In the higher income group, money is not itself a problem but brings associated problems in its wake. The leisure enjoyed by the upper socio-economic strata as a result of affluence causes problems. They are neither career-minded nor do they have much of a familial role to play because they have smaller families and any amount of paid help for running their homes. The proverb "An idle mind is the devil's workshop" is the phrase applicable to the situation this group of women face and this is the root cause of dissatisfaction in their married lives. They lack the proper attitudes or values, or a sense of a properly directed life.

In-law Problems

The in-law problem is an important factor in marital adjustment as is agreed upon by respondents of all socio-economic strata. In spite of all the advantages of a traditional joint family system, one loses freedom and independence in a joint family. That is why we hear our younger generation saying "The joint family system should go. Enough of joint family system! Every family should be on its own" etc. Mothers-in-law sometimes treat daughters-in-law with so much vengeance, that they make the latter's lives miserable. This results from a vicious circle created by socio-psychological causes. Since they in their time had received a similar treatment when they had come as daughters-in-law into the family, given the chance they display a similar adverse attitude towards their own daughters-in-law, gaining thereby an unconscious psychological pleasure.

33 per cent of the women of this study stayed in joint families, the rest in nuclear families. But surprisingly over 46% of the

women questioned had in-law problems. Even women in nuclear families, though living separately from their in-laws, frequently face interference. This is because in most Indian homes, even nuclear families are not rigidly compartmentalised units, as there is frequent interaction with relatives living outside the nuclear unit.

Sometimes the in-laws play havoc with the lives of a young couple even if the husband and wife are temperamentally compatible and are fond of each other. The case of Vimla, the purohit's daughter, illustrates this. She grew up in Calcutta, and after her marriage moved to Chidambarm where her in-laws live. She, being the eldest daughter-in-law, had to do all the domestic work for the 10 members in the family. Her mother-in-law and her sisters-in-law were in the habit of nagging her. They went to the extent of not allowing her to sleep in the same bedroom with her husband. Unable to bear such ill treatment she shunted between Chidambaram and Calcutta for five years. A complete separation was inconceivable since she belonged to a very conservative family. Her father himself was dependent on his two married sons and hence he too could not support her for longer periods. So her problem remains unresolved.

Other Reasons

Excess of family responsibility was found to be another predominant cause for marital maladjustment, particularly in the middle and low socio-economic strata. In a joint family, this reason exists more frequently. The wives are not given any time off to go out, and taking care of all the family members becomes a Herculean task leaving them no time nor energy for enjoyment. Besides, since they are compelled to do these tasks they derive no satisfaction from them. As a result, they feel frustrated. Only those women who accept it in the spirit of sacrifice might derive real satisfaction and might be able to make a happy marriage.

Sexual incompatibility was mentioned by respondents of all the three strata as a reason for maladjustment, but couples in the low socio-economic strata come across this problem more often than the others. On the whole over 30% of women who have been unhappy in sex found it difficult to make adjustments to marriage. Surely one big hurdle is won when a couple finds that they are sexually compatible.

The Indian woman readily adjusts her sexual and emotional

needs to those of her husband. Problems in marriage do not crop up unless there is serious temperamental and other differences which stand in the way of easy sexual adjustment and which in turn create marital discord.

Most women of the low and a few of the middle socio-economic strata do not have separate bedrooms for themselves. On the whole, nearly 30% of the women questioned do not have separate bedrooms for themselves. They lack privacy which comes in the way of sexual adjustment.

The husbands' lack of principles and questionable morals becomes a factor in marital unhappiness. Listen to what Sakun has to say. "Within a week after my marriage I knew I had married a dirty man. My husband had a women even before he married me which I knew only after it was too late. For no reason he would strike me on the face. Whenever I told my mother-in-law, she would shower abuses on me. Unable to bear the torture in my husband's house I ran away to my parents. My parents do not intend sending me back unless they are certain about my husband's behaviour. I am learning sewing and will earn my own livelihood. Marriage has brought me no happiness. If I am compelled to go back to my husband I will kill myself."

Married Life and Use of Tranquillisers

Marital unhappiness could be one of the reasons why women use tranquillisers. Often a person in anxiety starts on tension relieving drugs. This might gradually affect marital happiness through a slow change of moral values and psychological behaviour.

Drug addiction, which we occasionally come across in women of the high socio-economic strata, is practically unknown among the lower strata. However, the great majority of poor and middle class Indian women and even most upper class women do not use tranquillisers. On the whole less than 10% of women were using tranquillisers.

Mrs Singh, fairly happy in marriage, frankly admitted, "I am too tense to have a relaxed night with my husband unless I am on sleeping pills. I am basically a highly-strung person. What is wrong if I take pills to lessen my tension? This makes me less irritable and my husband more happy."

Naseema, a free-lance writer, was the typical example of a modern woman who has found release from her tensions in the world of drugs. "I have been on sleeping pills regularly for the last five years. I cannot say clearly whether my taking drugs coincided with loss of interest in my marriage. My husband and I really never got on well from the day we were wed. Marriage, instead of bringing us together, produced a chasm which widened each day. We probably did not click temperamentally. Each thought the other would change and honestly speaking neither of us is the type who would do so. I was very tense and had sleepless nights. The doctors started me on tranquillisers hoping to help me. Some of my friends showed me the panacea of the bottle. Now I cannot live without both."

Mrs Kiran, a doctor, boldly asserted, "Drugs have given me more happiness and peace than my marriage." Though Dr Kiran is still officially married, she works in Lucknow, while her husband, a professor, teaches in Delhi. Their two grown-up sons were abroad.

Though women have various reasons for taking tranquillisers it ultimately boiled down to one fact. A tense woman has greater problems in marriage and it is such a woman who takes to drugs to get a false sense of release from the world of problems, tensions, and frustrations.

Table 9

USE OF TRANQUILLISERS AND MARRIED LIFE

Married life		Use of tranquillisers		
		No		Yes
	No.	%	No.	%
Unhappy	57	7.20	12	13.80
Neutral	189	23.86	34	39.08
Happy	546	68.94	41	47.12
Total	792	100.00	87	100.00

Lack of sophistication and poverty have stood in the way of the wholesale acceptance of tranquillisers by urban men and women. But one factor which is paramount in keeping women off drug addiction and liquor has been their conservative background. The unmarried woman is not expected to drink or live on drugs. Once she is married, as a mother and wife she is expected to maintain a certain decorum. This has given the Indian woman a deep inner conviction that she has enough mental strength to face problems better than man who more easily accept the panacea of liquor, tobacco, or drugs.

Religion and Married Life

Religion makes at the most only a marginal difference in marital adjustment. Quite often a woman's ultra-conservative or religious beliefs or prejudices might make marital adjustment less easy.

Table 10

RELIGIOUS ATTITUDE OF WIFE AND ITS EFFECT
ON MARITAL ADJUSTMENT

Marital adjustment	Religious nature			
	No		Yes	
	No.	%	No.	%
Difficult	6	11.76	77	9.31
Neutral	9	17.66	202	24.43
Easy	36	70.58	548	66.26
Total	51	100.00	827	100.00

The ones having some difficulty in marital adjustment would naturally hold on more to God and religion in their crises and be influenced more by religious beliefs.

Kamala Joshi, hardly in her twenties said, "I can look only to God for help. My husband lost his job three months after marriage. Since then we have been in constant trouble. He is in terrible moods and everyone feels I have brought ill-luck to him. Realising the numerous problems marriage has brought me, I am now doing *sani vrata* to tide over these difficult days."

Usha Goel complained, "The main difference between my husband and me is that he is a *nastik* (agnostic) and I am very religious. He makes fun of me whenever I have a *puja* or *kirtan* at home. He objects to my fasting on Tuesdays. He need not believe in all this but he should not object to my devotional activities."

The wife's religious leanings is not very important as a single factor in marital incompatibility. The usual Indian household revolves around tradition and religion, though it is less ritualistic compared to earlier times. A girl who is not overly religious can have the same problems as a devout woman who lays stress on fads and fasts. The modern Indian woman has no choice but to make a compromise in her convictions to suit those of her husband if she wants a compatible marriage.

Though religion may be a major factor in the overall development and functioning of the Indian male or female, religion has not become a major deciding factor in adjustments two people make and their happiness. There are more significant factors like the individual's background, temperamental differences, in-law interference, economic status, the respect and freedom a woman enjoys to function as a wife, mother and working woman, her ability to give and take, listen and obey, and the time a man is willing to give to the marriage partnership. All these factors are the bricks for building up the pattern of a marriage.

Despite the diverse internal and external factors influencing marital adjustment and happiness, the majority of Indian mariages work out well. This is primarily due to the stable background of most man and woman which gives them a better start, the effort they make to maintain the familial institution, and their ability to overlook personal considerations for the stability of a marriage partnership.

THREE

Sex and Family Planning

There is no denying that sex is one of the prime forces behind innumerable human actions and reactions. But at no time in history has so much emphasis been put on sex as at present. Life is related in an intricate manner to the functioning of sex. Apart from the genuine effort which is being made in the scientific and clinical study of sex, there exists an obsessed and perverse attitude amongst lay men which stresses is the fact of sensual enjoyment as the most important experience of life.

Every human being, male or female, passes through various phases of sexual development from adolescence to old age. Sexual maturity at adolescence is preceded or followed by the sexual urge. In due course of time this longing for sex leads to hetero-sexual attachments in the great majority of people and results in sexual fulfilment. Every society provides for the natural growth and expression of various shades of sexual fulfilment within the framework of a marriage partnership. The biological instinct of sex had to be modulated to fit into a socially sanctioned marriage partnership because with the evolution of men, a new state was reached when the pleasure of sex was detached from its reproduc-tive purpose. Besides, when sex did result in conception and repro-duction the care of the offspring became a paramount considera-tion which could not be overlooked. The human child's dependence on its parents for the major part of its childhood made it impera-tive for sex to be given social and legal sanctions within a stable male-female partnership.

Even in primitive times rules were laid out to avoid indiscrimi-nate licence in sex. Sexual permissiveness was looked down upon

by most societies. Where it was allowed for certain religious practices, as among the African natives, the aboriginals of Australia,
the ancient Greeks, the Pharoahs of Egypt or among certain sects
in India, it was an extension of the supposed utilitarian effects of
sex in averting danger and promoting community welfare. Similar
reasons could be seen in fertility rites among various primitive
groups. As people became more civilised they dropped many of
these crude symbolic practices. Exceptions barring, men and women
gradually adopted a pattern of restrained and stereotyped sex
behaviour which was conducive to personal happiness and social
welfare.

Women's biology, being more intimately linked with maternal
functions, follows a different pattern regarding sex and sexual
satisfaction. She carries her biological role more intimately in her
physical makeup, temperament and moods. She has a definite on-
set of sexual maturity with menarche and an abrupt decline of her
biological maternal functions with menopause. The period between
menarche and menopause consists of over 30 years and is dominated not only by her sexual urges as a human being, but also by her
strong maternal instincts which often overshadow her sexual instincts. Many women are happier playing their biological role
rather than overindulging in sex purely for greater sexual gratification. This is because the effect on sexual behaviour of upbringing,
tradition and cultural background cannot be easily wiped out. They
leave deep furrows in the human psyche which are difficult to
erase. Keeping this in mind it would be worth understanding the
Indian woman's attitude to sex.

Sex Knowledge

Surprisingly enough over 60% of the women interviewed felt that
every woman should know more about menstruation, conception,
child-birth and family planning. Most women feel there is no harm
in girls acquiring knowledge about sex during adolescence.

This is Kantimati's view: "I grew up in a village and got married
at the age of 12. Till then I had led a sheltered life and knew
nothing about marriage, sex, or child-birth. My daughters are so
different. One is 20 and the other 18, both are not yet married.
They have been brought up in Bangalore. They read books, talk
to friends, and discuss sex with friends. I think that is the way it
should be. They could not live in ignorance like me. They belong

Table 11

KNOWLEDGE ABOUT SEX BEFORE MARRIAGE IN RELATION TO SOCIO-ECONOMIC CLASS AND EDUCATIONAL LEVEL

Responses	Less then primary		Middle & high		College		Professional		Total	
	No.	%	No.	%	No.	%	No.	%	No.	%
Upper										
No	2	100.00	23	74.19	69	41.07	5	14.28	99	41.90
Yes	—	—	8	25.81	99	58.93	30	85.72	137	58.10
Middle										
No	48	96.00	137	76.97	97	40.93	8	44.44	290	60.04
Yes	2	4.00	41	23.03	140	59.07	10	55.56	193	39.96
Low										
No	178	89.90	31	67.39	3	100.00	—	—	212	85.82
Yes	20	10.10	15	32.61	—	—	—	—	35	14.18
Total										
No	228	91.20	191	74.90	169	41.42	13	24.53	601	62.20
Yes	22	8.80	64	25.10	239	58.58	40	75.47	365	37.80
Grand Total	250	100.00	255	100.00	408	100.00	53	100.00	966	100.00

to the new generation. After all they must be made knowledgeable about sex to be able to protect themselves in a big city."

Mrs Jha, a scientific officer observed, "We cannot expect Indian mothers to plan their families if they are not educated about sex. Besides, a woman must know how to protect herself against veneral diseases or an illegitimate pregnancy." Mrs Jha felt sex education must form part of the school syllabus for senior students.

The small percentage not in favour of sex education for girls belong to the conservative group. Their argument is that sex education before marriage will make girls go astray. They feel sex need not be learnt. A women automatically knows about the facts of life after marriage. Many who believed in sexual restraint felt that there should be no hurry to give sex information before it was needed.

Over 60% of Indian women have no knowledge about sex before they are married. Knowledge about sex is closely related to social status and education. The better the social status, the better informed a woman is on sex matters. While over 58% women of the higher strata have knowledge about sex, only around 14% of women belonging to the lower strata have any knowledge of it. With education knowledge about sex increases, irrespective of the socio-economic structure. Educated women have greater access to sex knowledge through books and other literature. They are less inhibited and make an effort to learn the facts of life. Moral norms change and an educated woman feels that the better informed she is about such matters the more progressive she is.

Educated women from the lower classes find it more possible to break away easily from conservative patterns than women from a middle or high social strata with the same level of education. Women with moderate education in the high and middle strata generally come from more traditional backgrounds and maintain a certain reserve regarding attitude to sex and sex knowledge. But as education spreads the percentage of women having sex knowledge also increases in general (Table 11).

Sex knowledge before marriage, as claimed by one-third of the women, is usually speaking not very precise. They have not had a course of lectures on sex matters, nor have all of them read books on sex. More often it is knowledge they gleaned from friends, cousins, or acquaintances.

Vimla Sharma said, "All the knowledge I had before marriage was from friends. I knew that the sex parts of the male and female came together during coition. I also heard that, after marriage, a woman is expected to oblige her husband in bed and please him. But I did not even know how a baby was born."

Preeti Jain gave her account as to how she acquired sex knowledge before marriage. "Sex was never openly discussed in our house. We sisters discussed marriage and intercourse with friends rather secretively. On a few occasions, as young girls, my two elder sisters and I watched our neighbour and his wife engage in sex from a window on the first floor. We used to wonder what they were doing until one day our mother caught us watching the scene. Then it was mother who explained that it was very wrong to pry on others in their bedroom. What they did was part of marriage and we would know more about it when we got married."

In some Indian women there is not even a strong desire to know about sex. The feel the proper time to know about it is after marriage. Some even feel indifference and wonder if there is anything worth knowing before the wedding night. Most youngsters with education are less inhibited. They know about sex and are better prepared on such matters before marriage.

The average Indian woman is not over-enthusiastic about discussing sex. She feels there is a place and time for it and baring a very small percentage, they do not discuss it frequently with friends. More than half of the women we questioned never discussed sex with friends. In most Indian homes the subject of sex is taboo. A certain restraint is maintained on matters pertaining to it. Sex is not freely discussed by parents with their children, or between men and women, or even among friends.

Mrs Nalini Sastri, a lecturer in economics, said a woman who is busy with work and leads a normal family life has no time for such talk. Sex is a personal and intimate matter, and one cannot make it commonplace by discussing it with others. Any woman with a certain maturity of mind will not waste her time discussing sex.

When we consider less educated women in all the three different social groups, we find that women from the middle and low socio-economic strata are more frank than women in the higher group. Girls with a low educational level in the higher economic strata come from very conservative families where sex is never discussed.

Table 12

PATTERN OF FREE SOCIAL INTERCOURSE IN DIFFERENT SOCIO-ECONOMIC
CLASSES IN RELATION TO EDUCATIONAL LEVEL

Response	Less than primary		Middle & high		College		Professional		Total	
	No.	%	No.	%	No.	%	No.	%	No.	%
Upper										
Never	1	50.00	3	9.36	22	21.29	7	18.91	33	13.20
Sometimes	1	50.00	17	53.20	55	30.72	10	27.03	83	33.20
Always	—	—	12	37.44	102	56.99	20	54.04	134	53.60
Middle										
Never	19	38.00	50	27.32	33	13.25	2	11.11	104	20.80
Sometimes	27	54.00	99	54.09	125	50.00	9	50.00	260	52.00
Always	4	8.00	34	18.58	91	36.55	7	38.89	136	27.20
Low										
Never	55	27.36	10	21.74	—	—	—	—	65	26.00
Sometimes	120	59.70	28	60.87	1	33.33	—	—	149	59.60
Always	26	12.94	8	17.39	2	66.67	—	—	36	14.40
Total										
Never	75	29.64	63	24.13	55	12.76	9	16.35	202	20.20
Sometimes	148	58.51	144	55.18	181	42.00	19	34.56	492	49.20
Always	30	11.85	54	20.69	195	45.24	27	49.09	306	30.60
Grand Total	253	100.00	261	100.00	431	100.00	55	100.00	1,000	100.00

Discussing sex is not a common practice. Whatever curiosity one has in adolescence is satisfied by secretly talking about sex with a cousin or a friend or more rarely by reading a book or magazine. A woman's first practical lesson in sex comes with marriage. Many women have admitted their absolute ignorance about it before the wedding night.

MIXING WITH MEN

How free is the Indian woman with man? Does the conservative pattern of living, which is dominant even in cities, give women the freedom to mix with men? Is a woman mentally prepared to shed her inhibitions in the company of men? In the overall interrogation of 1,000 women, nearly half followed a middle course. They mixed with men occasionally. They said they were uninhibited with men who were close family friends or near relatives. They had no special interest in mixing with various types of men. It was not expected of them nor had they any desire to do so (Table 12).

Mrs Chowdhury, who comes from a fairly conservative family, said that when her husband's business acquaintances or personal friends come home she stays away. Only when very close friends or near relatives come do she and the other women in the house join the menfolk in conversation. Even this is a great leap forward for Mrs Chowdhury. In her mother's time a woman did not enjoy such freedom. The women in the family observed purdah and there was no question of women sitting with men and chatting or enjoying a joke in their company. Mrs Chowdhury did not observe purdah but always covered her head in front of her elders, both men and women.

Over 20% of the women stated definitely that they never mixed with men. They did not know the company of any man other than their husbands, brothers, younger brothers-in-law, or fathers. Male company is taboo as it was not customary for women to mix with men. Women have to be contented with female companions. Once a girl attains puberty she stops talking and mixing with boys. Even with close male family members she has to observe a certain decorum and distance. More than 30% however had no problems in mixing with men, whether it was at a function, a dinner, or a visit to a friend. They joined the company of men without reservations.

Sanchita, a second year college student, said that in her grand-mother's time girls of her age hardly ever mixed with boys. She comes from a well-known traditional Bengali family where, till two generations ago, women observed purdah. It was a sign of sophistication for a woman to keep female company. Now it is the other way round. Progressive women mix with men. In her family a daughter now enjoys as much freedom and liberty as the sons.

The pattern of mixing with men is closely related to the socio-economic status and educational level of a woman. The better her status the more at case she is with men. From over 53% of women in the top category who mixed freely with men, the figure drops to 27% in the middle social strata, and to 14% in the lowest strata.

Education brings another significant change, for with better education a woman sheds her inhibitions. Her family, if it is pro-gressive, encourages her to mix with men and women. There is a definite correlation between the pattern of mixing freely with men and the educational level of a woman. This correlation is noticed in all the socio-economic stratas.

Women at all levels of society with college level education are most outgoing. They take full advantage of their freedom and social liberties. In general, such Indian women have no reservations about mixing.

DISCUSSING SEX WITH THE HUSBAND

Sex is seldom discussed by a woman even with her husband. At a higher social level, however, there is no taboo and what is read in books, what is seen on the screen, or what happens in one's own sex life or that of others is often the subject of conversation.

Table 13 shows the close relation between the freedom a woman feels in discussing sex with her husband and her socio-economic background. The average Indian female does not particularly relish discussing sex. Sex is a personal habit which she might or might not enjoy. She is more interested to know about pregnancy and child-birth. The idea of discussing intercourse, even if it be with the husband, appears new and strange.

Table 13

DISCUSSION ON SEX WITH HUSBAND IN THE DIFFERENT
SOCIO-ECONOMIC CLASSES

Discussion on sex with husband	Socio-economic class							
	Upper		Middle		Low		Total	
	No.	%	No.	%	No.	%	No.	%
Never	34	16.18	164	38.57	198	88.79	396	46.42
Sometimes	140	66.67	217	51.05	24	10.71	381	44.66
Often	36	17.15	44	10.38	2	.50	76	8.92
Total	210	100.00	425	100.00	224	100.00	853	100.00

Mrs Anand expressed her dislike of it thus: "What is there to talk about sex? Words do not increase the enjoyment. Its pleasure is spontaneous and it has to be treated that way." Many women said they felt embarrassed talking about it with their husbands. Mrs Mani was of the opinion that sex is not a subject to be torn to shreds. Many things in sex are just understood, not taught or learnt.

Mrs Hingurani said that when they were much younger, she and her husband sometimes did talk about sex but not now, after 15 years of marriage.

Mrs Kamal Kaur a middle aged Punjabi woman put it aptly: "For me and my husband sex is for pleasure, not for talking."

Kanti Ma, a domestic servant, gave a loud laugh when asked whether she spoke to her husband about what gave her enjoyment or him pleasure. "What is there to say?" she said, "Only fools would waste their time talking about what others do in bed and what one does oneself."

Rani Bai appeared hurt when she was asked whether she talks about sleeping together with her husband. "We may be poor but we are not vulgar," she said. "We talk about the children, the money, need to buy the ration, or the meal to be cooked, but sleeping together we never discuss."

Younger women, especially the educated, said that they were absolutely free with their husbands and discussed sex without any embarrassment. Mrs Dey, a young bride said, "My husband asks me after intercourse whether I felt an orgasm. He has even asked me to describe what I feel. I make sure that he enjoys what happens to me by talking to him freely." Vimi admitted her ignorance "My husband does most of the sex talking. I just listen. After all he reads more than me."

The great majority go through the sex experience spontaneously. They do not analyse the experience. Sex is something to be enjoyed, not a subject for academic discussion.

ATTITUDE TOWARDS SEX

Every woman accepts sex and over 30% have healthy attitudes and enjoy it thoroughly. Sex and its enjoyment are a part of growing up from girlhood to maturity and motherhood. The less sophisticated the female, the more unquestioning she is about sex. Her responsiveness is determined by the demands of the male and there is usually a synchronisation between the two.

Attitude Towards Sex and Education
    With the educational level improving there is a sudden change in women's attitude to sex. The modern female is becoming increasingly conscious of her expectations and fixes a standard to be achieved. The natural urge is replaced by certain fixed ideas she may develop about what she wants from sex. The table below shows a definite correlation between sex interest and the educational level of the respondent.

Table 14

ATTITUDE TOWARDS SEX IN RELATION TO EDUCATIONAL LEVEL

Attitude	Educational level									
	Illiterate & primary		Middle & high		College		Professional		Total	
	No.	%	No.	%	No.	%	No.	%	No.	%
Unfavourable	97	41.81	47	20.00	38	10.32	4	8.89	186	21.13
Neutral	100	43.53	127	54.04	172	46.74	24	53.33	423	48.07
Favourable	35	14.66	61	25.96	158	42.94	17	37.78	271	30.80
Total	232	100.00	235	100.00	368	100.00	45	100.00	880	100.00

When Sharada, a mother of four, was asked how she revealed to her husband her inclination for sex, she laughed and related a very interesting episode. "One afternoon I was reading a Hindi novel and suddenly felt very excited. I took the book and went to my husband and showed him the page. He smiled and understood me." When we asked what happened, Sharada blushed and replied, "What had to happen happened. My husband took the hint and walked with me to the bedroom."

When women of the lowest educational level say they are not at all interested in sex, it reveals their passive approach to such a relationship. When they were asked whether they showed any desire to sleep with their husband, nearly 42% said they had no special desire, against 10% of educated women who were indifferent to sex. The unlettered, simple woman gives what the man asks or wants. It is not for her to bother how much she is inclined towards the act. It is her husband's need which must be fulfilled. As most women with less than primary school education come from the lower classes, their preoccupation with domestic chores engulfs them. They have no servants to help them. They are in monetary distress and most of the time in or just out of pregnancy. For these women belonging to the lower strata of society who have no idea about family planning methods, sex means another pregnancy and delivery. This fear of repeated child-birth removes most of the charm of sex. Poor health is another major factor which decreases a woman's interest in sex.

Kaushalya, a Bengali mother of six though hardly in her thirties, said she was least interested in sex. She slept with her husband because he wanted it. She dreaded another pregnancy as her health was very poor and her husband's income as a peon was insufficient to run the household. In such cases the struggle to exist takes priority. Sex becomes a matter of routine about which the woman has very little choice.

Joythirshree, a midwife, had no interest in sex for other reasons. She was sterilised so she did not fear pregnancy but with two grown up girls and a job she had many other things to preoccupy her mind. She has occasional sex with her husband, purely to oblige him.

Among educated females, those with a college level education are most interested in sex and its various ramifications. They are aware that sex is as much a woman's concern as a man's. Among women with college level education, nearly 43% declared that they were interested in it. The educated woman is able to enjoy intercourse as much as her husband. When there is greater communication between man and wife and more understanding, interest in sex grows. The woman is less scared of unwanted pregnancies as she is better informed about family planning methods. And the woman who comes from a more enlightened strata of socity has more leisure for enjoying a full sex life.

Table 14 shows a drop in the professional woman's desire for sex. Preoccupation with professional interests, outside jobs, domestic responsibilities, and often a lack of time sap her energy. She is less enthusiastic because of her multifarious preoccupations. Non-professional educated women are more likely to be carried away by romance notions created by advertisements, women's magazines and modern fiction. There is an acute desire in such women to live up to the sex ideals created in the west, and they search for something which is always elusive.

The average illiterate female does not display any such interest, for her sexual behaviour is something as natural as eating or suckling an infant. When her husband needs her, she is aroused. She gives in. Sometimes she enjoys it and sometimes she does not. But she does not stop to think about sex.

The educated woman's attitude to sex changes because of her intellectual involvement and her desire to get more and more out of the act. Sex, she feels is not a routine but something from which she and her partner can drive great joy by greater understanding and better methods. With education, sex, thus becomes a volitional act aiming at maximum enjoyment. It is important that every educated woman realize that it is not the quantity of sex that matters but the richness of the experience.

Attitude Towards Sex and Age

Among Indian women, interest in sex decreases with age. Most men and women after some years of marriage gradually come to a convenient understanding. With the early romantic years of marriage receding and newer responsibilities and concerns coming into life, the two subconsciously assign a secondary place to sex. It often happens that if the man and woman are of religious temperament, the process of giving precedence to other family obligations becomes relatively easy.

Fig. 11 shows how from 38% in the 15-24 age bracket the percentage of women showing interest in sex drops to 8% in women over 45 years. The Indian woman passes through the various stages

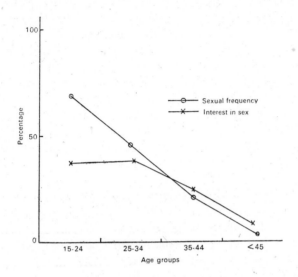

Fig. 11. Interest in sex and sexual frequency in relation to age.

of life from menarche to marriage, motherhood to menopase with few emotional upheavels, as her obligations as mother frequently override other considerations. She matures gracefully after marriage. Her concern for her family and children often gets priority even over her sex life. With an increase in age a woman's expectations change, and enthusiasm for sex decreases.

Mrs Sud indicated how during the first few years of marriage sex was very much a part of her life. Practically every other day or sometimes daily she had intercourse with her husband. He was the passionate type and could never get a good night's sleep unless he had sexual release. Now, sometimes even weeks pass without sex and she does not seem to miss it so much. Very often, due to heavy pressure of work, her husband is too tired to make any advances to her at night. She too has more domestic work, with four growing children, which completely exhausts her.

The Indian woman's cultural upbringing is such that sex forms only one of the many factors that bind her to her husband. With age and many years of marriage, the sex urge wanes and other values acquire importance.

It is, however, interesting to note that at all age levels half the women remain interested in sex. In the youngest age bracket the majority are always interested in sex. Thus we see that, unlike her western counterpart, who is often neurotic about sex, the Indian woman takes a more sober attitude. The gurus of the West further aggravate this abnormal attitude by declaring that sex enjoyment and orgasm is a woman's prerogative at all times. She is openly advised to seek the man who will fulfil this requirement, or to resort to autoerotic methods to achieve greater sexual satisfaction. Hormonal treatment is widely used to ensure rejuvenation. With this obsession for self enjoyment the average woman of the West is all the time chasing a mirage.

Attitude Towards Sex and Occupational Status

The woman who takes up employment is more progressive. She takes an active interest in all her personal achievements including sex. She gets greater opportunities for meeting men than a house-wife. She is more exposed to sex magazines, literature and uninhibited conversations. However rarely do Indian woman display overt interest in sex.

When considering a lack of interest in sex it was surprising to find that many more working women showed a lack of interest in sex than housewives. While only 19% housewives were not interested in sex, 27% working women said they were not interested in it at all (Fig. 12). Perhaps, the interest of working women gets divided due to multifarious preoccupations.

The conflict between professional work and family obligations may be marked in some working women. If they have no help at home their anxiety and frustration affects their sex life. Some working women are so career-oriented that they consider an interest in sex as sentimental and frivolous. If a woman has an unhappy marriage because of her job, she develops a negative attitude towards sex.

The working woman has greater chances than the non-working woman of getting romantically linked with men before and after marriage. If the working woman has met with a serious disappointment in love her attitude to sex becomes coloured by it. Madhumati, who was working as a secretary, developed a strong dislike

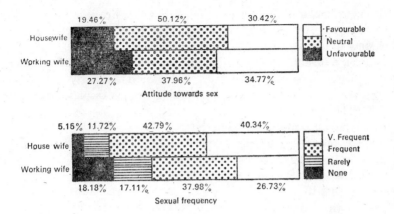

Fig. 12. *Attitude forwards sex and sexual frequency in relation to occupational status.*

to sex because she had loved and lost. "Love and sex are the greatest obstacles a girl has to overcome when working because men are always eager to exploit working girls. I have come to hate men and sex because of my own experiences." Housewives are more balanced in their attitude as over half of them fit into the in-between category of being moderately interested in sex.

Attitude Towards Sex and Married Life

Though marital happiness is related to the interest a wife shows in sex, it is worth noting that over 46% of women who are happy

Table 15
MARRIED LIFE AND ATTITUDE TOWARDS SEX

| Attitude | Married life | | | | | | | |
| | Unhappy | | Fairly happy | | Happy | | Total | |
	No.	%	No.	%	No.	%	No.	%
Unfavourable	40	65.57	67	31.45	75	13.04	182	21.43
Neutral	11	18.08	119	55.86	268	46.60	398	46.87
Favourable	10	16.35	27	12.69	232	40.36	269	31.70
Total	61	100.00	213	100.00	575	100.00	849	100.00

in marriage are only neutral as far as their sex interest is concerned. Another 13% of woman who have no interest are also happy in marriage.

In the healthy woman, interest in sex is a true index of her happiness in marriage. However, only the moderately interested get the most out of marriage. When a woman displays excessive libido her marital life becomes less happy than in the case of a woman who is moderately interested.

Mrs Jagadesh's case is a typical instance. She felt she was very sexy and passionate unlike her husband who was matter-of-fact and reserved. She said she was fed up of being the active partner for the last 10 years of her married life. She was convinced that her warm character in contrast to her husband's reserve in sex matters was the cause of marital tension in her life.

Mrs Bose, a sprightly young lady in her early twenties, also had a similar grudge against her husband. "I am more interested in sex than my husband. Most of the time he is tired or too concerned about his office problems. In fact my husband does not fully satisfy me. But I am not the type who will go round looking for fun. I know he loves me very much though he is not able to satisfy me."

Sex is one of the many factors contributing to marital happiness, and even those women who are not fully satisfied realise this. In this the Indian woman shows an unusual maturity of character which allows her to consider the other values of life as well. Mrs Amrit explained how her values in life had changed out of necessity. "I used to be interested in sex but not any more. I have learnt to take an interest in many other things and find happiness in them. My husband gives me everything, except sex. About five years ago he lost his sexual strength. It may be related to the fact that he is a diabetic. Though I have not enjoyed sex for the last five years, I would say my married life is happy. We are building a small flat. He is extremely nice and obliging to me and my daughters. We go once in two years to Punjab to visit my parents. And when time permits, I do a bit of sewing and knitting for others. I do not think I am an unhappy person because I do not have any sex. After all, don't I have the love of my husband and children?"

This strength of character is something unique in Indian women. They have a tremendous capacity for overlooking personal problems in the interest of others. This is something which they do not as an obligation, but as an inner conviction that is part of their mental makeup. In view of this attitude, one begins to wonder at the exaggerated importance given to sex in certain societies. A little rethinking is necessary, for they have to assign sex its proper place in human relationships.

SEXUAL FREQUENCY

For an Indian couple sexual closeness is not the only or the strongest factor in a marriage partnership. Though it plays a very vital role in maintaining the charm of the early years of marriage, it unobtrusively takes a less important place as more and more responsibilities enter married life. The concept of excessive sexual indulgence as an index of marital harmony is not accepted by most Indian couples. Romantic love, which dominates the concept of male-female relationships, especially in the West, is often subordinated to other considerations among Indian couples.

Sexual Frequency in Relation to Age

As age increases, the frequency of sex for the Indian female diminishes. From over 70% of women in the age bracket 15-24 years who have intercourse three to five or more times a week, the percentage drops to about 47% in the 25-34 age bracket, to 20% in the 35-44 age group, and to a low 2% in women above 45 years of age. Fig. 11 shows clearly that sexual frequency is directly related to age in the case of most Indian women. Around 80% women have frequent sexual intercourse.

In spite of the sexual restraint which comes with the increase in years more than one third of women over 45 years have sex from once a week to twice a month. Over 60% of even the elderly have sex occasionally, though sexual frequency decreases with age and as the marriage advances.

Mrs Mallick laughed when she recalled that during the first few years of marriage she and her husband had coitus practically every day. Now it is different. Though their love for each other has grown, interest in sex had dwindled. She could attribute this only to the numerous responsibilities that had come into their lives plus the fact that they were both growing older.

The decrease in sexual frequency as a marriage accumulates

years is often accepted in a natural way. Mrs Puri put it jokingly, "When the children are as tall as we are, how can it be possible to have sex every other day? We would be mad to think of it." Mrs Sondi, mother of four, said that she went to her husband at least 10 days in a month as otherwise her husband became very irritable and shouted at people. However, irrespective of the decrease in desire with the advancement of age which women usually experience, they normally adopt a pattern of sexual frequency which suits the husband's likes and temperament.

Sexual Frequency in Relation to Occupational Status

Housewives have sex more frequently than working women (Fig. 12). Preoccupation with work gives the working woman less time for the demands of marriage. The work itself, commuting to and fro, and the lack of domestic help physically and mentally tires a working woman, and she is often left with no energy for sex.

Mrs Narasimhan works as a clerk in the railways. She explained her problem. "It so happens that half of the days in the week my husband is tired and exhausted. When he is in the mood I am too tired and fagged out. So days pass without our having slept together. We only blame the complicated life which we all have to live." Some working women are too independent in thought and action to give in easily to their husband's wishes. The housewife who is completely dependent on her husband economically is liable to comply more readily with her husband's wishes. This brings a big change in routine sex life.

For the housewife, sex enjoyment becomes an important diversion and she looks forward to a night with her husband. She accepts sex in marriage as an integral part of the partnership without questioning. A working woman, who plays a multifarious role, has to adjust her married life to her other interests and diversions.

Other Factors Affecting Sexual Relations

In some cases, external factors prevent a normal sexual relationship between husband and wife. Some women mentioned that due to lack of privacy they seldom had sex with their husbands, more so in a joint family with insufficient accomodation or where the woman was frequently separated from her husband due to his being away on work or employment. In such cases sexual frequency in even a young couple was infrequent. Kanaka, though married for over a year, said she could not have had intercourse with her husband more often than once a week. He felt that frequent sex was debilitating. Mala's problem was different though not unusual. Married six months ago she must have had intercourse with her husband only a dozen times. Her mother-in-law thought her son was too young to be a father and she did not allow Mala to share a bedroom with her husband.

The fear of pregnancy for many illiterate couples removes the charm of sex, and they deliberately abstain to avoid pregnancy. Some conservative men and women practice sex control as a part of religious discipline. There are certain days in the week or in the month when they do not indulge in it. Probably in no other culture but ours is abstinance considered a virtue to be practised to enhance one's physical and spiritual powers.

There are also certain unusual situations where sexual frequency is reduced in a woman due to her sharing her husband with another woman. Asha Gupta's is such a case. Her husband married her because his first wife could not bear a son. Asha narrated her story. "Bhabiji and I are friends. We live under the same roof with one husband. We even have fun at night deciding whose turn it is to go to his bedroom. I usually sleep about 10 times a month with my husband." There were more instances of women sharing their husbands with another wife.

SEXUAL SATISFACTION

Most Indian women are satisfied with sex—36% always and 58% sometimes. It is also interesting to note that 38% of women who do not find satisfaction continue their marriages although adjustment is made more difficult on that account. Unlike their Western counterparts who make a great issue of it, 25% of those who never get sexual satisfaction do manage the other adjustments easily. This speaks a lot for the Indian woman's healthy attitude to sex. However, now with greater freedom, opportunities, physical comforts and privacy, marital adjustment is becoming more difficult.

As seen in Table 16 there is a definite correlation between marital adjustment and sexual satisfaction. Though there are numerous other factors which influence adjustment, a happy sexual partnership forms the basis for happy marriage.

Table 16

SEXUAL SATISFACTION AND MARITAL ADJUSTMENT

Marital adjustment	Sexual satisfaction					
	Never		Sometimes		Always	
	No.	%	No	%	No.	%
Difficult	35	38.04	33	7.48	4	1.33
Somewhat difficult	34	36.95	122	27.21	41	13.71
Easy	23	25.01	286	65.31	257	84.96
Total	92	100.00	441	100.00	302	100.00

Mrs Pinki Lal complained, "My husband does not even bother to find out whether I am satisfied. He cares only for his own needs. How could I be happy in marriage when, from the very first week my husband showed no consideration for my needs. When he wants it, I have to give in. If he does not, I will just have to go to bed and sleep." Usually women are satisfied with whatever they get. They feel that sexual satisfaction is a man's prerogative. It is their duty to give in to their husbands' pleasures, whims and fancies.

Mrs Banerjee is unhappy in marriage because she hardly gets sexual satisfaction and this has caused tension. She said, "My husband enjoys oral sex because he is not satisfied in the normal way, and I give in to him with disgust. This has stood in the way of compatibility in marriage."

Mrs Jha could never adjust to her marriage because of her dislike of sex. "I have never enjoyed it with my husband because he likes to have sex only after a drink and I cannot even stand the smell of alcohol. I have obliged my husband mechanically for the last six years without getting any pleasure." Though some women go through the semblance of sex with their husbands, such women can be deeply hurt when then the man compels her without regard to her needs. Bakul's story was a typical one. "How can I enjoy myself with my husband. I know he comes to me only when he has no other alternative. He keeps a woman much older than me and goes to her regularly. When he is broke and has no money, he comes to me. I hate to sleep with him. I have never known any happiness in marriage."

Some women, even if their sexual relationships are not satisfactory, compromise and find the other kinds of happiness that come with marriage. Exceptional women efface their personality so completely that they think only of their husbands. Mrs Bajaj was one such. She remarked, "I feel most happy when he is satisfied." Such women, who have completely renounced their feelings and think only of their husbands can be happy in marriage in spite of not enjoying sex in the usual sense of the term.

FAMILY PLANNING

Family planning is an integral and vital part of our present economic programme. Our national policy aims at making family planning a way of life for people of every region, community and religion. In this context it is worthwhile knowing the Indian woman's attitude, since it is the deciding factor in planning a family, even though all kinds of persuasive efforts are being made by the government. After all motivation is stronger when it comes from within rather than when it is imposed. A woman will be truly liberated only when she can rationalise her view on family planning and decide and act upon them.

The importance of family planning increases when we consider that there are over 100 million couples in the reproductive age and each one of them could contribute towards the success of the programme. A woman makes a greater biological cotribution to a marriage partnership as she gives birth to and nurtures the child. So her attitude to family planning assumes great significance. Sometimes women might not be in favour of raising more children. Imposing on them more responsibilities than they can handle is unfair. At times women are deserted by their husbands if the financial burden becomes too heavy for him and this leaves the family in a worse situation. According to medical reports, no mother can remain healthy if she has to bear the burden of too many pregnancies in quick succession. Producing too many children without being able to give them adequate protection and care is cruel and is a real injustice to them. Instead of spending valuable human resources in taking care of children with an inadequate budget, the same could be invested in the more productive developments of individuals, society and the nation. The practice of family planning has far-reaching effects. Apart from the interest of the individual, it should also be practised in the larger interest of the community and the nation.

ATTITUDE TOWARDS FAMILY PLANNING

Though family planning has been given official recognition since 1951, active undertaking of the programme started only a decade ago. It is encouraging to note that the idea of family planning has been sold to the average Indian woman. The attitude of a woman to family planning is influenced to a certain extent by age. The percentage approving of family planning decreases as the age group increases. But acceptance is about 2/3rd among even the older age groups. This clearly shows that, irrespective of age, the great majority of Indian women approve of family planning (Fig. 13). In our survey the percentage of women who do not approve of family planning is less than 10% in the 15-24 age bracket. The figure increases with age to reach 36% in women above 45 years.

Innumerable reasons were given for favouring family planning. Economic distress in which the urban poor and middle class live seemed the most pertinent reason for desiring it. The immediate thought was, if there were more children, it would be impossible to bring them up well, considering the limited income of the family.

Kavita puts it in a nutshell. "When we cannot feed even the three children we have, why should we want more?" Vimla Devi said, "I have six children. Now times have changed. With the soaring prices of essential articles people cannot bring up their two or three children. I compelled my eldest daughter to undergo the operation to stop child-birth after her third delivery." In the urban culture, as the joint family system is breaking up, many women from nuclear families face the difficulties a woman experiences in bringing up children. Servants are a problem, and there is no help from the in-laws or one's own mother. Space is often limited and most commodities including milk are scarce. Many of the women were concerned with the immediate problems of bringing up large families.

A few women in the younger age group favoured family planning so that they could take up employment. A desire to limit the family's size so that wives could contribute to the household budget was expressed by a few women from even the lower strata of society. Devi, a maid-servant who does part-time work in two households, said she could not afford any more children. She already had a boy and a girl who were being looked after by her elderly mother when she went out to work. If she had any more children she would have to give up working.

Some women felt their health suffered after repeated child-births. Middle-aged women who had more than four or five children often gave this as one of the reasons for approving of birth control. Contrary to popular belief, even the urban poor do not want many pregnancies. Their economic distress is so great that they realise life would become even more difficult if the family increases in number.

The ones who did not favour family planning, though few, had very strong objections. "We cannot go against the wishes of God" was Mrs Pantulu's remarks. Mrs Desai, the eldest woman in a large joint family, opposed it strongly. "All this family planning is nonsense. If a woman does not bear children what is her purpose in life? If we go against the laws of nature we will have to face the consequences." Some women, both in the younger and older age group felt family planning was harmful to health, and a few mentioned religion for their aversion to family planning.

A few women, especially in the older age groups, adopted a passive attitude. "If I am destined to have many children, I will have them. If not, I will not have them. Why should I bother about it?" was Virbala's remark. "We will have what God gives us" was Mrs Agarwal's dispassionate reply. She was the mother of 10.

For the young, family planning is a very vital issue and they were intensely concerned about it. The older generation was inclined towards passive helplessness. The only encouraging feature was that, even though some of the older women had not planned their families and had large numbers of children, they wanted their daughters to have fewer children and adopt birth control methods.

Younger women, though more favourable towards family planning, were not necessarily very well informed about the methods. They had heard about family planning and had reasons for limiting the number of children but did not know how to go about it. Many women said their husbands did not seem as much concerned as they were about this problem.

The average woman, though in favour of having a smaller family, was not clear about what she ought to do and which method

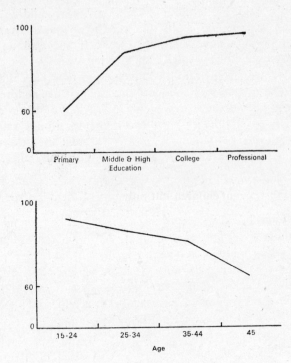

Fig. 13. Attitude torwards family planning in relation to educational level and age.

would be best for her. As the educational level improves, the women adopts a positive approach to birth control. She recognises that family planning will not only improve her family condition, it will lessen her domestic duties and will give her greater latitude for functioning outside the confines of her home.

Mrs Poddhar, a lawyer living in a joint family, stated vehemently, "Most of the women in our family practice planning. All of us have only two or three children, and we have all been able to do a lot outside the home as working women or as social workers. I do not think we could have achieved this if each of us had six or seven children like our mothers and grandmothers. Family planning is the first step to a woman's emancipation." Fig. 13 shows how acceptance to family planning is directly related to education.

40% of women with primary school education or below do not

favour family planning. If education increases to even middle school level, the percentage drops to 14%. This shows that education brings a drastic change in the attitude to family planning. Given a poor family planning education the woman remains conservative and is full of superstitious beliefs and false fears. Her ignorance is one of the greatest obstacles towards the better life she could enjoy by practicing family planning.

Among the poorer sections of our society, the woman is generally illiterate. It is in this group that the infant mortality rate is high. Hence women with low education, especially in the lower strata of society, are reluctant to accept family planning for the fear that their children might not live. Rukku, a lower class woman said, "I have delivered eight children but only one of them is alive. I would like to have one more son. How can I stop having children? My husband will take another wife. We poor people have no money to fall back upon and only our children will feed us when we are old."

Some women with low educational standards even mentioned that children were necessary to help them in their family business. The washer woman, Meerabai, said that her family was fairly well off because she had four sons who were all working with her husband. Her point was what was the need of birth control for poor people who made a living with their own hands. They believed that the economic status of the family improves by having more children, especially boys, who are looked upon as an investment in human resources.

THE PRACTICE OF FAMILY PLANNING IN ACTUALITY

Though over 80% of the women we interviewed approved of family planning, the women who actually practised it constituted only about 45% of the sample. The lower the social strata, the more ignorant a woman is about family planning methods. From over 75% in the high socio-economic strata the percentage comes down to 56% in the middle and then to 19.5% in the lower socio-economic group (Table 17). This is very significant when we consider that women in the low and middle strata should be more effectively covered by family planning methods than those who are economically better off.

Hari Priya, right in the heart of Allahabad, was the mother of five children. Her husband, a painter, earned less than Rs 300 a

Table 17

PRACTICE OF FAMILY PLANNING IN RELATION TO SOCIO-ECONOMIC CLASSES IN DIFFERENT REGIONS

Responses	Regions											
	East		West		South		North		Central		Total	
	No.	%	No.	%	No.	%	No.	%	No.	%	No.	%
Upper												
No	14	30.43	11	22.91	9	19.56	6	16.21	14	31.81	54	24.43
Yes	32	69.57	37	77.09	37	80.44	31	83.79	30	68.19	167	75.57
Middle												
No	50	54.34	32	35.55	39	43.33	42	46.15	34	40.47	197	44.07
Yes	42	45.66	58	64.45	51	56.67	49	53.85	50	59.53	250	55.93
Low												
No	36	75.00	32	69.56	39	82.97	41	83.87	42	91.30	190	80.50
Yes	12	25.00	14	30.44	8	17.03	8	16.13	4	8.70	46	19.50
Total												
No	100	53.76	75	47.54	87	47.54	89	50.30	90	51.72	441	54.85
Yes	86	46.24	109	52.45	96	52.46	88	49.70	84	48.28	363	45.15

month. She was frightened that 'an operation' to stop child-birth would be harmful to her as her health was not good. Her husband was also unwilling to undergo any operation. She did not know what else she could do.

Tara, a sweeper and a mother of four, repeated more or less the same story. She herself did not want more children but she was helpless in the matter as her husband just did not bother. She did not know what she should do.

Kherunnisa had gone through eight child-births and had four living children. She dreaded another pregnancy as her health was bad and it was so difficult to run the household with what her husband earned. She would readily do anything if she could stop having children. But she too seemed helpless in the matter.

Though there is no great difference, area-wise, in the practice of family planning as seen in Table 17, the upper category on the whole shows greater awareness to family planning especially in the north, south and west regions. Among the middle class the western zone scored higher in comparison to other regions. In the lower lot west again showed an increased awareness to family planning. While 75% of women in the upper category practice family planning, only 50% of the middle and 20% of the lowest strata resort to it. This emphasises the need for approaching the low and middle strata for imparting knowledge about family planning techniques.

Table 18

DISTRIBUTION OF COUPLES BY NUMBER OF CHILDREN

Number of children	Percentage distribution and couples with children (Housewives)	Percentage distribution of couples with children (Working wives)	Percentage distribution of couples with children (All)
One	24.86	30.64	26.54
Two	37.57	32.32	36.20
Three	19.23	14.46	18.23
Four	7.62	9.25	8.04
Five	3.63	3.47	3.49
Six	3.98	6.35	4.42
Seven	1.27	1.75	1.34
Eight	1.84	1.75	1.74

Considering the total sample, only 45% of them practice the known techniques. About 10% are above 45 years of age and thus may not need family planning. But the rest of the 45% have to be covered by this scheme.

Table 18 shows the distribution of couples and the number of children. About 75% of these women need to adopt family planning techniques either to space the arrival of the next child or to stop further child-births. Once the number of children has crossed the maximum of two, one needs to follow the scheme more strictly, as once couples have large families the addition of one or two more makes no difference to them.

DIFFERENT FAMILY PLANNING METHODS

The family planning methods mentioned by respondents were the pill, withdrawal, sheath, sterilisation, vasectomy, loop, rhythm and diaphragm. The sheath and the pill seem to the most popular among the high socio-economic group, the withdrawal method and then the sheath among the middle socio-economic group, and sterilisation was found to be preferred in a few cases of the low social strata.

Operations for family planning were not very popular among the socially well placed, as this group knew other methods of birth control. The sheath and the pill were the most favoured. Many women mentioned that they used more than one method, depending on the circumstances, availability, and the mood of the moment. It is interesting to note that about 7% of even the high social strata practiced the undependable withdrawal method.

Among the middle strata withdrawal topped the list as the most popular method alone or in combination with the rhythm or the sheath. Then came the sheath or condom used by the husband. Sterilisation and vasectomy were not readily accepted by this group. Sterilisation is adopted by women of the low socio-economic class as they are not familiar with other methods. There was not even one case of vasectomy mentioned in our survey. A few were on the pill which was given by the employers in whose homes they were working.

Subha, an ayah, said, "For the last three years I am taking a tablet every day to prevent pregnancy. Memsahib took pity on me as already I have three children and sent me to her doctor friend who gives me the medicines." Muwa Raj, a driver's wife, said that her husband's employer gave her the medicine which she took daily for three weeks every month. After her third child she plans to undergo the operation to stop pregnancy.

In spite of the great eagerness among even women of the poorer sections, not more than one-fifth of them are covered by family planning techniques. They usually live in ignorance. Often it is due to lack of opportunity, privacy, co-operation from the husband, or just laziness. We have still a long way to go to implement the family planning programme on a war footing so that every couple to whom the idea is sold will be able to adopt the method best suited to them.

In addition to its importance in checking the population explosion, family planning helps to improve the overall status of women. There is an old Arabic proverb, "If you want to keep your wife at home, keep her pregnant and do not get her a pair of shoes." A woman who goes through repeated deliveries throughout a major part of her life from adolescence to menopause, shines only as a mother and a wife, confined to the four walls of her home with its problems, joys, rewards and tribulations. Unless a woman is able to limit her family to a reasonable size, she cannot play an all embracing role in the home, the community and society. Family planning has ushered in a new era for the modern woman. Not only does it improve family welfare and social prosperity, but it is essential for individual happiness.

With the number of reproductive couples increasing every year, an overall effort has to be made if substantial results are to be achieved in birth control. Though the idea of family planning is accepted by the average woman, there is a wide chasm between its acceptability and application, especially by the lower sections of society. Educated women of the upper and middle social strata, who are more conscious of the importance of birth control resort to it without governmental incentives or compulsion. But in the lower strata, the majority of women are not able to help themselves because of ignorance, poverty, and often the husband's indifference. More often it is the non-availability of a proper advising agency rather than any serious objection to the idea that prevents women from taking to family planning. Hence to be really effective for the underprivileged, the campaign has to be linked with the availability of family planning means. All the methods should be explained so that individual requirements can be met. Unless all facilities are taken to reach the message to the poor, the depressed, and the illiterate, there is bound to be an unhealthy imbalance in the birth rate of the different socio-economic groups with the gap between the privileged and the underprivileged widening even further.

FOUR

The Generation Gap

A mother has tremendous influence on her children, especially on the daughter in a traditional society like ours. A girl, by the time she reaches adolescence, realises that it is this image she has to emulate and in her own life desires to be a wife and a parent like her mother. This stereotyping of girls often starts at a fairly young age. The way a girl behaves, the way she dresses, talks, walks, eats and even sleeps, falls into the pattern set by her parents, the family and the community. The modern environment, however, being highly individualistic, competitive, bold and uninhibited, gives each individual the freedom to be different from set patterns of social norms.

The type of upbringing a girl gets, her education, training in the fine arts, the freedom to move without restraint, the taboos imposed on her, and the privileges she enjoys determine what she will be in the future. Will a daughter be an exact prototype of her mother in her opinions, actions, behaviour and emotions, or an individual with original views on life and living?

The generation gap is nothing new. The younger generation has always been divided between its loyalty to the old and its inner convictions that the new trends set by the changing pattern of the society are better. The more rapid the change in the environment, the wider the gap. At no time in history has the generation gap been so great as in the latter part of the twentieth century. The affluent, industrialised countries of the world have mostly faced the brunt of it. This is because of the uprooting of families and immigration to urban complexes, breaking up of the joint family system, the discarding of traditional values, devaluation of marriage and the loss of religious belief. Modern industrialised societies have such diverse elements in every group that every individual deviant can find a place somewhere. However, the feeling of alienation increases because of the individual's decreased sense of belonging.

In a less industrialised group, if it is traditional and conservative, family oriented, and interdependent, individual transformation is slower. But even a less industrialised country like India has seen significant economic and social changes in the last 25 years. The status of women has changed. There is strong disapproval of dowry, *purdah*, caste discrimination, child marriage and various other social evils. Every educated individual, male or female, gives thought to these issues. The more enlightened a person is the quicker is his mental transformation. He or she hopes for positive change in the society. The moneyed elite is more prone to attain the cultural pattern of the affluent and materialistic West at the cost of one's own intrinsic culture, values, and beliefs. This change is specially evident in the young, educated rich.

Young people of today, especially in the urban higher economic sector, are well informed, independent in outlook, and affluent. They want to chalk out their own futures with less parental guidance. They want to break away from everything traditional and conventional, and blindly ape western modes of dress, life-style, tastes, aspirations and even behaviour. This often leads to a great conflict between the generations unless the parents also undergo a similar transformation.

How wide is the gap between the parent and the daughter in a typical urban group? Has the older generation shown a capacity to change with the times? What patterns are set for the daughters? These are vital questions and their answers will reveal the truthful picture of the typical girl productive of the current urban Indian culture.

INTERACTIONAL PROBLEMS WITH PARENTS

In the present investigation very few daughters had serious conflicts or a strained relationship with their parents. When all the different socio-economic strata are considered, only an insignificant percentage admitted to discord. Nearly 70% of the women had no parental problem and the rest fit into the in-between category of having occasional disagreements with mothers and fathers (Table 19).

Table 19

INTERACTIONAL PROBLEMS WITH PARENTS IN DIFFERENT
SOCIO-ECONOMIC CLASSES

Interaction problems	Socio-economic Classes							
	Upper		Middle		Low		Total	
	No.	%	No.	%	No.	%	No.	%
Never	151	60.40	356	71.20	186	74.40	693	69.30
Sometime	91	36.40	137	27.40	57	22.80	285	28.50
Always	8	3.20	7	1.40	7	2.80	22	2.20
Total	250	100.00	500	100.00	250	100.00	1000	100.00

The lower socio-economic group appears to have less interactional problems with parents. Occasional interactional problems increase with the rise in the socio-economic status. In the upper strata daughters are exposed to many more opportunities with the freedom and time to avail of them. They emulate their peers in their outlook and activities. Consequently their expectations and demands are much more than those of their elders or even their less fortunate counterparts. This leads to differences of opinion with parents.

Snehalata's case illustrates this point. She was the only daughter of an I.A.S. officer and had been allowed great freedom from her childhood. She enjoyed liberties that her mother had been denied when she was a girl. At college she fell in love with a boy whom she wanted to marry. When her parents heard that the boy was the son of just a junior company executive, they objected to the marriage in spite of all their modern ideas. Against the wishes of her dear parents she married the man she loved and even after six years the misunderstanding with her parents has not been patched up. Her relationship with them remains strained.

The better the socio-economic status, the greater the freedom the daughter enjoys, but in spite of progressive ideas, parents often expect their children to conform to the pattern set by them. When it comes to a serious decision like choosing a profession, marrying, or joining an academic course, the parents often want to have the final say in the matter. In many cases, because of the strong parent-daughter relationship, the girl gives in readily. But if the daughters have had a very independent upbringing conflicts arise when views diverge. However, in the middle and low socio-economic strata, parent-daughter conflicts are fewer as the daughters are less independent in their outlook and actions.

About 30% of women in the entire group conceded having occasional problems with parents, though many stated that it did not seriously affect their relationship. The most common conflicts centred around dress, going out with friends, wanting to continue studies, desire to take up employment, love affairs, orthodox practices, etc.

With better education the interactional problems with parents increase. While 77% of women with less than college-level education never had problems with parents, only 50 to 60% with college or professional education can make the same claim. This shows that with better education, parent-daughter views diverge, resulting in a wider gap.

In spite of education, however, and despite the improvement in social status, most Indian women have cordial relationships with their parents. This is because of the strong family ties which bind a daughter to her parents no matter how different she may be from her parents. The daughters as children are dependent on their parents for their well being and they give due respect to the opinions of parents. They abide by their wishes in most instances. Often the parents themselves avoid crises. Whether the adjustment comes from the parents or from the daughter, problems are minimised.

Restrictions Imposed by Parents

Most women feel that their parents are neither too strict nor too liberal. They allow them to enjoy freedom for certain things but put restrictions on other matters. More restraints are imposed by parents on daughters in the lower socio-economic strata, but as social status improves, parents themselves become more liberal.

The less educated a family is and the lower its socio-economic status, the greater its insistence on girls being brought up to fall into the traditional pattern. After maturity and till marriage a girl is chaperoned so that there is very little chance of her going astray. If she does go astray, there is no question of compromise, she is completely disowned by the family. As most girls in the lower strata get married fairly early, the period of waiting till marriage is very short. The picture changes when the girls are from better-off families and are themselves better educated. The more progressive a family, the more it is concerned to provide daughters with better opportunities in a competitive world. These girls, having enjoyed greater freedom, become very independent in their outlook and wish to live the life of their choice.

Often in the higher socio-economic groups parents themselves are busy with their social commitments, and the children are left on their own or in the care of servants. Often, in order to enjoy greater freedom themselves, parents give greater liberties to their children. Sudha, in the first year of college said, "I always have freedom to do what I like. Most evenings my parents are not home. They are either at the club or visiting friends. I go to the homes of my friends to watch television or stay home listening to music. Even if I entertain boy friends, my parents raise no objections."

Meera Saxena, married with three children, said she was brought up without restrictions as both her parents were working and they did not encourage her to be too dependent on them. Throughout her schooling and college years she was in the hostel and never knew parental restriction. During the three years prior to her marriage, she was allowed to do whatever she liked as they felt she was old enough to take care of herself.

In India however, those brought up without any parental restraint are more often the exception that the rule, even in the higher strata mentioned above. Over 75% of women are usually brought under parental restrictions and abide by them (Table 20).

Table 20

RESTRICTIONS IMPOSED BY PARENTS ACCORDING TO SOCIO-ECONOMIC CLASS

Responses	Upper		Middle		Low		Total	
	No.	%	No.	%	No.	%	No.	%
Never	56	22.40	107	21.40	23	9.20	186	18.60
Sometimes	144	57.60	229	45.80	104	41.60	477	47.70
Always	50	20.00	164	32.80	123	49.20	337	33.70
Total	250	100.00	500	100.00	250	100.00	1000	100.00

Many women of the higher socio-economic strata mentioned that parental interference and restrictions came only when they did something drastically wrong. Most of them said they knew they had to keep to certain rules and behave with responsibility. Hence they never really got into trouble with their parents and the question of interference did not arise.

Nearly 80% of women in the middle socio-economic strata come under parental restrictions. They accept it without grumbling and justify the right of parents to control the liberties enjoyed by their children, especially girls. Mrs Vittal, a library clerk's wife said, "There was no question of taking extra liberties with our parents. We girls in the family knew how much freedom we could take and never took undue advantage. Our parents did not have to impose restrictions on us as we did not expect more liberties."

In her role as a daughter the Indian female is willing to abide by certain restrictions because she is a girl. She is conditioned not to exploit the few liberties given to her, hence she can avoid constant conflict with her parents by accepting by and large the restraints imposed on her. She probably intends doing the same thing with her daughters.

In the low socio-economic strata, over 90% are brought up very strictly. Because of the great value attached to virginity a girl's chastity is guarded. Once she is married, the responsibility is passed on to her husband and his family. In the lower strata, if a woman is sexually immoral, it usually starts when the marriage fails.

These days, with the increase in employment opportunities and educational facilities even girls belonging to the low socio-economic strata are enjoying greater freedom. Arati, in her twenties, worked as a household servant for over five years before her marriage. She said her parents imposed restrictions on her going out late in the evenings to meet other people working in the same building or to chat here and there after work. But they did not object to her wearing nice clothes, going to a cinema with her girl friends, or even going out of Calcutta once with her master and mistress and their children.

Neelam, a village girl, took up employment in the city to support her ailing father, mother and three sisters. Her parents did not object to her living alone in the city with unknown people since her aunt was living close by and kept an eye on her. Then she got friendly with the chowkidar and planned to marry him. Her parents come to know about it, and took her back forcibly to the village. There she was married to a different man belonging to their own community during the same summer. After 15 years she is back in the city again with her husband who is now working as a peon in an office.

Most parents, especially in the lower socio-economic strata, express great concern about settling a girl in life once she has attained puberty. She is considered a liability till her marriage. Restrictions are imperative for the upbringing of girls. Most girls accept this and fall into a certain pattern of behaviour marked by modesty and restraint.

Kantamma, a bangle seller's wife, justified the restrictions her parents imposed on her. "After puberty we girls could not even go out and stand on the outside veranda. Now I follow the same pattern. My daughters, though they have been brought up in Madurai, do not know the streets beyond our neighbourhood. We cannot allow our girls to go astray, as we see in films. For us a girl's character and prestige are more important than anything else."

A girl enjoys freedom till she reaches puberty. A few years after marriage, she may move around again without too many restrictions. Kanchanlatha, a gipsy girl, said the day she menstruated she stopped going around selling beads. Six months after her marriage, she restarted the rounds with her gipsy husband. In their community they did not believe in exposing girls after puberty.

Change in Outlook between Generations

The Indian woman is passing through a transition more so if she belongs to the younger age group, is better educated and is of high socio-economic status. In general women's outlook does not differ much or at the most differs only occasionally from that of their parents. On the other hand, in all cases, the difference of opinion with parents decreases with age. The percentage of women who often differ with their parents is over 9% in the age group 15-24. The percentage drops to around 3% in women over 45 years old (Fig. 14).

Women in general have not undergone a revolutionary change in outlook from that of parents. They conform more readily than disagree. But the tendency to differ is clearly perceptible. Although less than 10% differ from their parents completely in their outlook, about two-thirds claim to have occasional disagreements with their parents even in the different age brackets. Women having an outlook similar to their parents are concentrated in the older age group (more than 45 years old), those who have less than high school education, and also in the lower income group. The reverse is true for the younger, educated and upper income group.

It is observed that the generation gap has existed in every generation even in a tradition-bound society, as in India. When a South Indian from a conservative family two decades ago gave up wearing a saree in the caste style she considered herself very progressive, or say when a Rajasthani or Kashmiri girl 20 years ago stopped covering her head in front of strangers she took a great leap forward in comparison to her mother. Similarly women of every period have shown some change in outlook and habits. However, the last decade has seen a drastic change in outlook. The young people of today are better informed but rather misguided and confused in their hurry to change. Many of them are hybrids of two different cultures which have no meeting ground. They accept alien habits and denounce native ones as "uncultured and primitive". This creates a break from the life pattern and opinion of their own parents.

Figures 15 and 16 show the change of outlook brought by better education and improved socio-economic status. The more educated the person and higher the socio-economic status, the greater is the difference with parents. Even when these three factors operate, only about 10% are complete non-conformists. This is very significant, as it shows that even in an urban culture the Indian women of today have not made a complete break from their parents.

We have seen that women of today have not changed radically from their parents. The parent-daughter bond is so strong that daughters respect the parents' views and abide by them. 65% of Indian women always abide by the wishes of their parents. Only in the upper socio-economic strata the percentage drops to 53% (Table 21). These women with their better education opportunities and improved economic conditions become more independent in their outlook which prompt them to take their own decisions although it might contradict the views of their parents. The upper group of women score higher than the middle and lower even in case

Table 21

ABIDING BY PARENTAL WISHES

Abiding by wishes of parents	Socio-econonic Class							
	Upper		Middle		Low		Total	
	No.	%	No.	%	No.	%	No.	%
Never	11	4.40	20	4.00	9	3.60	40	4.00
Sometimes	105	42.00	135	27,00	69	27.60	309	30.90
Always	134	53.60	345	69.00	172	68.80	651	65.10
Total	250	100.00	500	100.00	250	100.00	1000	100.00

of having occasional protests against the wishes of their parents.

A greater percentage make their own decisions though it contrasts with the wishes of others.

The independent outlook fostered by better education, improved status and greater opportunities brings about a change in women, and leads to conflicts with family members. Sometimes the importance given to individual freedom in thought and action is over-stressed at the expense of every other consideration. When

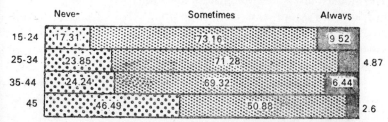

Fig. 14. *Difference in outlook between parents and daughters in relation to age.*

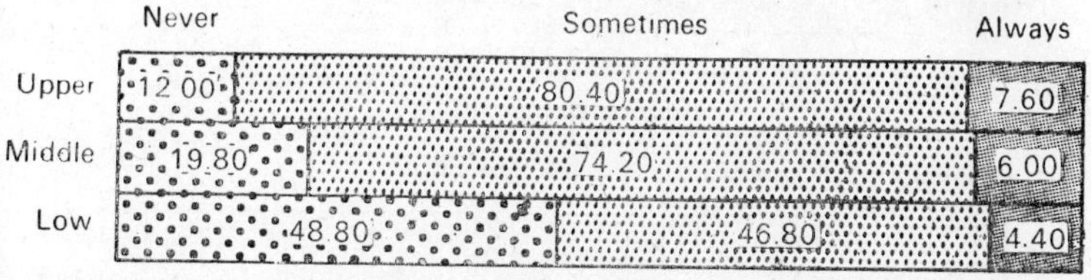

Fig. 15. *Difference in outlook between parents and daughters in relation to socio-economic status.*

the modern young woman in the name of freedom of choice flouts all parental authority, problems between the generations become acute. As seen in Fig. 14, while in the younger age group, around 17% never differ in their opinion from their parents, in the older age group nearly 50% never differ. Hence even negatively speaking this shows the change that is coming over younger women.

Change is a necessary element for progress. Change in ideas, views and behaviour signifies a dynamic social progress. But change for the sake of change which does not help in social reformation and has no bearing upon the cultural milieu is meaningless. Unfortunately, it is this type of change that is overtaking the modern young women of today. Those who belong to high society as a privileged lot enjoy greater opportunities and better facilities. Their parents are also more progressive and put less restraints on them. This modern young class complies least with the other social groups and is responsible in widening the generation gap. The low socio-economic group lags far behind the upper class because of lesser opportunities and more parental restraint. The middle group bridges the gap between the two.

EDUCATION FOR GIRLS

The modern urban environment in a socially developing country provides for more and more opportunities for the education of girls in various fields. Unless the attitude towards traditional practices changes, the facilities available will not be fully exploited. What is the woman's view on education? To what level must girls

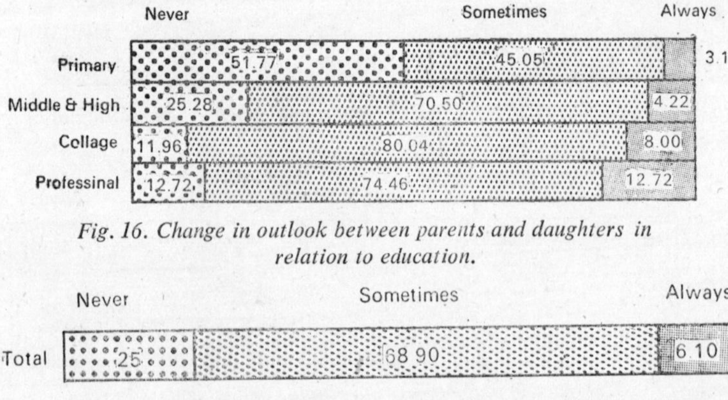

Fig. 16. Change in outlook between parents and daughters in relation to education.

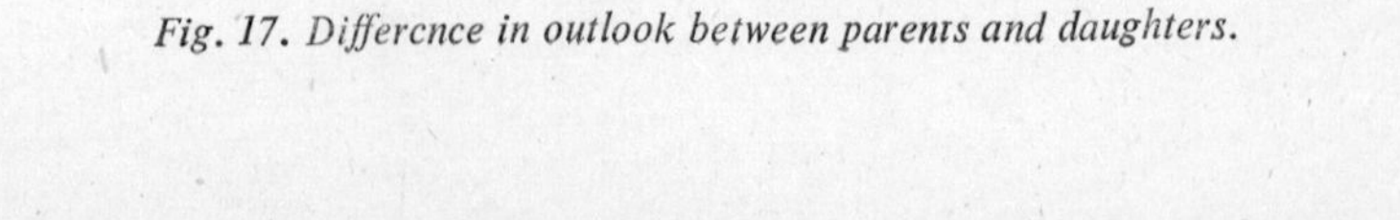

Fig. 17. Difference in outlook between parents and daughters.

be educated? Can sex education be given to them? What is their attitude to co-education? What extra curricular training should girls get? These questions must be resolved in order to determine the role of women in society in the future.

Socialisation of daughters is determined in two ways by the home environment and formal education. In general, higher education for girls is not favoured because it is thought that they are eventually to be married off and are not expected to support the family. Once married, their obligations are transferred to the husband and his family, except in unusual cases. However, in the upper socio-economic group slightly more than 50% would like to give daughters advanced training because they are in a position to do so as well as accumulate enough money for dowry. In the middle strata over half the women would like to give their girls training up to the college level, while in the lower classes more than 60% want their girls to be educated only up to high school. Upper class women from the north are an exception in that the majority expect their daughters to be educated only up to college.

Generally, as the socio-economic status improves, expectations regarding the daughters' education are also higher. This shows that the opportunities given to daughters has a direct relationship with the family income.

Some parents are fastidious about sending their daughters only to women's institutions. In the present study, it was found that about 66% of them are favourable towards co-education while the rest are unfavourable. The least reservations were found in the upper socio-economic group, followed by the middle strata while the lowest economic groups showed the greatest resistance to it. The educational level also determines the attitude of women towards girls in co-educational institutions. The higher the educational level, the more favourable is the attitude. Fig. 18 reveals that a favourable attitude towards co-education is directly related to the educational level of a woman and her socio-economic standing.

Jeeth Kaur, a well educated woman, explained "I do not mind my daughter studying in a co-educational school. A girl will not go astray just because she is studying with boys. A girl's character depends more on the upbringing she gets at home."

Maragatam, the priest's wife, got her daughter admitted to a local school which was co-educational. Maragatam asserted, "I have no objection to my girl studying with boys. I have not studied beyond Class V. I grew up in a small town and was married before 12. My daughter cannot end up like me. She will study further whether she is in a boys' school or a girls' school."

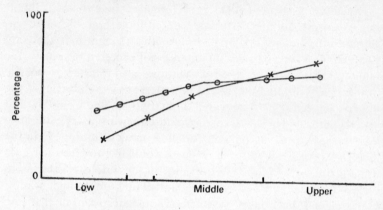

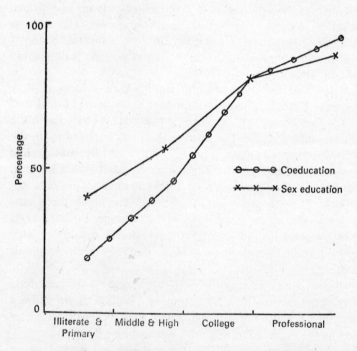

Fig. 18. Approval of coeducation and sex education in relation to socio economic status and educational level.

Surprisingly most women are broad-minded about co-education, and feel that as long as they get proper education, it is insignificant whether they attend girls' schools or mixed schools.

EXTRA TRAINING FOR GIRLS

Selection for the type of training girls should receive depends to a large extent on the socio-economic status. While the low income group opts for music as the first choice for extra training for girls, women of the middle and upper class strata consider dancing and tailoring more important. It is surprising that less women in the higher socio-economic strata consider training in music essential for girls. Only the middle groups of south and central India show extra preference for music. Even this is much less in comparison to the percentage of women in the low socio-economic group who prefer music. Painting as extra training for girls appeals only to a small percentage of women in the upper socio-economic strata in the East, South and West and in the middle socio-economic strata in the North.

When we consider a woman's views on extra training for girls in relation to her educational level we find the more educated a woman the less she considers music as a necessary qualification for girls. Less than 4% of the better educated opted for music as an additional training. Their approach becomes essentially utilitarian. Artistic pursuits are given less importance, especially by the professional women of the higher socio-economic strata.

The educated women at the college level both in the higher and middle strata show a wider interest in fine arts such as painting and dancing, along with a more utilitarian pursuit like tailoring.

The instinctive love for artistic pursuits is more evident in the humble and low than in the sophisticated and rich. Most Indians are familiar with the harvest songs, and the boat songs which women sing while drawing water from the well or while sowing seeds. Music is part and parcel of poor people's lives. Their appreciation of beauty, as seen in the *rangoli, alpana* or *kolam* in front of even humble hutments is ample proof of their fondness for design and colour. Their spontaneous desire to choose artistic training for girls especially in music and painting is a true expression of their love for the beautiful.

SEX EDUCATION FOR GIRLS

Educated women of the upper and middle socio-economic groups are in favour of imparting sex knowledge to girls in adolescence, though the low income group is more orthodox. They feel that matters regarding sex need not be told to children as they will learn about these at the appropriate time. On the whole approximately 60% are favourable towards sex education for children though most of them specify that information should be given only when boys and girls are sufficiently mature (Fig. 18). Even educated women are against thrusting such knowledge on children before they are ready for it. Overexposure to sex in childhood many fear might produce sexual permissiveness as in the west. Many women, however, show concern safeguarding girls against sex exploitation in urban living. They felt boys and girls could no more be brought up oblivious of sex matters.

Chitra spoke from personal experience. Being the only daughter of a very conservative family she could not frankly talk about sex to her parents. So great was her ignorance that she thought that if she touched a man she would become pregnant. Her own daughter now is so different from her. She is absolutely frank in discussing sex and is more mature and sensible for her age than her mother ever was.

The present study revealed that two-thirds of the entire sample was practical in their approach to this question. If sex education is introduced in higher classes in schools to keep girls better informed they saw no harm. What they disapproved of was the overexposure to pornographic literature and books which they felt would distort the growing minds of children.

Salima, the liftman's wife, remarked, "After all a girl is going to be a wife and mother. What harm is there if she learns about what happens after marriage or how a baby is born?" Indian women of different social strata have shown a positive approach in their attitude to girls. They have compromised on many issues whether it be education of girls, co-education, sex education, training in fine arts or giving girls opportunities to grow without excessive parental restrictions. Even in the selection of a husband for their daughters, parents usually take into consideration the likes and dislikes of their daughters. This shows that damage to the parent-daughter relationship is avoided by the more liberal approach to girls in all the different socio-economic strata. This in combination with the gradual transformation that is taking place in the younger age group has helped lessen the generation gap in most families even in the present decade.

FIVE

Socio-Economic and Cultural Aspects

The Indian woman, whatever may be her status, sees herself primarily as a mother, and considers this role the most significant one. Whatever she does or whatever she achieves is an extension of this primary image. A woman's life is determined by the demands of her children. Being a mother is the most challenging, exacting and time-consuming task a woman faces during her lifetime. For several million years, man has been the hunter, going from place to place, fighting and gathering food. The change from a food-gatherer to a food producer took over 300,000 years. All through this long period of evolution and even later during the last few thousand years of stable agricultural life, woman has been the child bearer, the preserver of the home, and the custodian of the children. Woman as the mother image, the *Ma*, the personification of Mother Earth is a deep rooted idea in any primarily agricultural society. Urban encumbrances and modern responsibilities have not been able to eradicate this basic concept of woman.

Mrs Billimoria, a business magnet's wife and a full-time housewife, felt that women lose their dignity and standing when they forsake their responsibilities as mothers in order to accomplish other things. On the other hand, if they could take in their stride different obligations and yet fulfil the tasks of motherhood, that would of course be a much greater achievement altogether.

Even woman who had significant achievements in other spheres did not look down on the mother image. Mrs Patel, a leading lawyer, said, "If I am a woman, successful professionally, it is because of the love and affection I get from my husband and children. It is their love that gives strength to my personality. Since my primary needs of a mother are satisfied, I am able to carry out other responsibilities." Except for the women of the higher category in the Eastern region, the upper and middle South Indian group and the middle strata in the Central zone, the rest gave the first rank to the mother image. Though many observed that they had to be wives before they became mothers, they seemed to identify their role in life with being a mother rather than a wife.

Mrs Wadwani, a school teacher, said, "My emotions seem to sway more with the joys and sufferings of my children than with my husband. Not that I love him less or any such thing. It is only that most of my responsibilities as a woman seem to centre round the children."

Women as mothers are willing to accept difficult situations, make greater adjustments and undergo numerous sacrifices if necessary. Only in their role as mothers are they willing to subordinate all other considerations. They are unable to overlook the interests of their children even for the consideration of their husbands. Mrs Mishra, a widow who lost her husband when she was hardly in her twenties, never thought of remarriage because of her concern for the children. She felt her obligations as a mother to her children was greater than her personal desire for a marriage partner. With a sense of pride Mrs Mishra said, "I'm not sorry for not having remarried. The joys and duties as a mother have been more rewarding."

The Indian woman has had a fairly stable socio-cultural environment in spite of the serious political, economic and religious upheavals the country has gone through. Though the woman has played a subordinate role to man, she is respected as a mother. Her standing as *Ma* or *grihalaksmi* was venerated by society and religion. She has been inspired to sacrifice all other considerations and even personal interests in order to maintain this ideal image. This has left a permanent impression on the character of the Indian female, who unlike her western counterpart regards her role as a mother to be a revered and elevated one.

In all the socio-economic groups in the different areas except the upper strata of the East, the upper and middle groups of the South and the middle strata of the Central region, the role of wife was given second rank. For most women marriage and the role of the wife was only a stepping-stone to the fulfilment of their life's ideal, i.e., motherhood. Though most admitted their primary duties as a wife, they were unwilling to give it a greater importance at a cost of their roles as mothers.

Those who conceded the role of wife as superior than that of mother felt that the partnership with a husband continued for a life-time while the motherhood became less important when children grew up and settled down in their own lives. Anasuya Bhat clearly pointed out: "When I married I did not have children. Now I am forty-five and have no children living with me. My duties as a mother were important but my primary role in life was that of a wife; the mother role is second to it in importance." Chitra Govind, wife and mother said, "I became a mother after having been a wife, hence my duties to my husband are greater to me than any other role in life." Career consistently stands third in role preferences. Though most women see the importance of a career even after marriage, they are unable to subordinate their domestic duties to the demands of a career. Exceptions barring, Indian women give their careers relatively less importance.

In the West, with the advent of the machine age, jobs which were solely a women's domain were taken over by machines and gadgets, whether it be grinding, husking, milking the cow, churning butter, mending or weaving a rug. As they were relieved of these duties women began to feel that they did not contribute to the economy of the society. As mechanisation increased rapidly the clear division of labour between men and women ceased. Women stepped into men's occupations in order to prove their worth.

The desire to be educated and eventually get trained for a career exists in most women. But there is no rigid or compulsive attitude towards a job or career. Given the opportunity, time, and training, many might feel an inclination to take up work outside the home. On the whole women are also more prone to overlook taboos and restrictions and enter a career. But they do not want to jeopardise domestic comfort or convenience even for the sake of personal recognition, emancipation, or a sense of fulfilment which they might get by taking up an independent occupation or profession or even a vocation.

Role of Women in Decision Making

The pattern of roles provides for a definition of what is to be done in a family, who is to do it and who is to decide on the allocation of tasks. The roles of family members tend to be determined according to sex, age, and other factors peculiar to the cultural patterns of a particular group. Work in and about the home is done more often by women and girls than by a men and boys. Men usually play the instrumental role of providing finance and take on themselves the main responsibility in making final decisions concerning major family problems. But as the status of women changes by their being more educated and getting employed, they are made to play a greater part in decision making. Hence many definitely have a say in family matters, although in the family hierarchy the relative power of the woman increases with age. In the matriarchial families of the South women take the major responsibility in decision making unlike patriarchal families. Recent studies show that women primarily and sometimes entirely make family decisions regarding the purchase of food for family, child care, buying of clothes and furnishing and participating with the husband in major financial expenditure and investment policies.

Table 22

EXTENT OF WOMEN'S PARTICIPATION IN FAMILY MATTERS

Participation in family matters	No.	%
Never	64	7.31
Sometimes	428	48.85
Always	384	43.84
Total	876	100.00

The present study shows that only less than 10% of women do not have a say in family matters (Table 22). The rest have always or sometimes voiced their opinion in family decision making. In more than 40% of cases, women have a definite say in matters concerning finance, children's education marriage etc. It is interesting to note that of those who have a say in family matters it is found that 80% have satisfying family relationships.

The Task of Meal Preparation
Cooking is a source of joy to many women. One can confidently

say most Indian women enjoy cooking as much as arranging flowers, weaving a basket, or embroidering a saree. It also gives scope for spontaneity and freedom of choice in the preparation and selection of the day's menu. The quantum of enjoyment a woman gets from cooking is naturally related to the interest she shows in it. Modern amenities like cooking gas and electrical domestic gadgets make kitchen work less tedious. However, these facilities, available for the urban rich, are not within reach of the poorer sections of society. Yet most women like to cook. Those who never like it are negligible.

The lower the socio-economic level, the greater is the number of women fond of kitchen work. With improvement in the socio-economic status and with better facilities more and more women fall in the category of enjoying cooking sometimes. Cooking is almost completely the woman's responsibility in all Indian homes. However, with improved social status, women get the help of servants who decrease the domestic work load. In spite of this more than half the women of the upper strata in the different regions except the west and south enjoy cooking only sometimes. There are various reasons for the top category women taking to this work less enthusiastically. The culinary art has passed on to the hands of cooks who have become a necessary part of any well-to-do family. Women keep themselves busy with other interests and when they are employed, it is understandable that their interests get divided between work and domestic duties.

Many, however, are preoccupied with beauty care, card playing, shopping, or socialisation. In many homes of the upper socio-economic strata, even children are looked after by an ayah or maid servant. Mrs Bhalla of Delhi remarked, "I hate cooking. One cannot expect a woman to waste her time in the kitchen when there are so many other things to do. I have a Bihari boy who makes the meals. I spend my time entertaining friends, going for bridge sessions or seeing movies in the afternoons. Only when there is a party do I step into the kitchen to give a hand in the cooking." To cook occasionally has a prestige value for high society women. They take lessons, try new recipes, learn to bake and preserve foods. Some like to impress their guests by fixing a fancy dish on a party day.

In all the areas except the East, the middle strata is composed of over 60% who always enjoy cooking. In the East, especially in Bengal, it is customary to assign the kitchen duties to a cook or *thakur* even in middle class families, in spite of the fact that a Bengali woman is fastidious about cooking.

Most women have no choice but to like cooking for they have few other preoccupations. To cook, shine the utensils, make pickle, and prepare papad is as much a part of her daily life as having a bath, suckling the baby or feeding her husband and children. The thought of not liking cooking is alien to her. Even the rural woman's work in the fields, husking or pounding, is done as an extension of her primary responsibilities as a cook. In the urban poor the picture changes a bit. Though 72% always like cooking we have about 25% who like to do it only sometimes. There are reasons for this.

If a woman is working as a dish washer or as a sweeper or a vegetable vendor she has to plan her day according to the whims and interests of her mistress or to suit the timings of her customers. She cannot be too preoccupied with domestic work. She may even find the daily routine of cooking a nuisance if she cannot find extra help.

One other factor which may decrease a poor woman's interest in the kitchen is the non-availability of essential commodities like kerosene, firewood, coal, oil, flour, etc. Every day starts as an ordeal and ends as one. If a woman is over burdened with many children, is in poor health, and facing monetary distress, her rejection of cooking may reflect her helpless state.

Krishna Bai had this to say about cooking "Madam, it is a nightmare for me to cook a day's meal. My husband does not give me money for the daily ration. He drinks and gambles while I slog the whole day. I work in four houses. My day starts at 6 a.m. and ends at 1.30 p.m. in the afternoon. Again I start work at 3 p.m. to end work at 6.30 or 7 p.m. in the evening. How do you expect me to like cooking? My eldest daughter who is 10, cooks a little rice. With whatever left overs I get from the houses where I work we manage our meals. One can enjoy cooking only when one has something to cook with." In spite of all hardships the great majority in the low socio-economic group likes cooking. Especially in the East, some women of the high socio-economic level attach much value to being disinterested in cooking.

TYPE OF FAMILY

A majority of women of this study lived in nuclear families. About one-third of the sample still had the traditional joint family set-up. Our culture ensures that everyone is helped by their immediate family of orientation or relatives when in trouble. Even though we have a large percentage of nuclear families, family ties are very strong among the network of families under one ancestry, and one finds these different sister nuclear families behave like a joint family in times of need and also for festive occasions. Actually speaking, these nuclear families are only extensions of the initial family set-up. There are several cases of extended families with the husband's brother or sister staying with them even after the death of the parents.

Over 60% of women in the sample preferred nuclear families which consisted of husband, wife, and their children. The percentage for both working wives and housewives was the same. They wanted more independence in their own homes and hence did not relish having the in-laws with them. Those used to joint families before marriage opted for the joint family set-up and the same was true for those used to living in nuclear families. There were cases of opposite views also.

Some of those who live in nuclear families become narrow in their outlook and were not always sympathetic to the needs of relatives. Mrs Bina said, "Doctor, you do not know the problems of joint families. One has always to adjust to another's convenience. If I have to go out for anything or even visit my parents, I have to get prior permission from my in-laws. My husband also has to abide by the wishes of his parents, otherwise there is likely to be chaos in the house. When I wanted to work in a school my in-laws created havoc. They said that I cannot avoid household responsibilities. They felt they had shouldered the domestic load for years and now it was my turn."

Indira Vakil felt that "there is no room for any compromise in a joint family system. One has to just give in always. One's turn comes only after the mother-in-law's death. That is a long time to wait for." Usually the revolt against the joint family system prevails only in the initial years of married life. Afterwards many women become part and parcel of the family and are well accepted by everyone. Then they start liking the interdependence in the joint family.

In Indian families parents look after children with utmost care. The emotional ties are so strong that they would like to live with their children throughout their life. When children grow up and become economically independent, the onus of taking care of their parents falls on them. This is an accepted pattern.

The respondents were asked about their preferences in living with children when they were old. Although some women do not like the joint family, they would like to stay with their children when old. The average person thinks only in terms of what is advantageous to himself. Those staying in joint families preferred staying with children in old age more than those living in nuclear families (Fig. 19). Some women from nuclear families preferred to stay with their children in old age. Mrs Shanta always lived in a nuclear family, even when she got married. After her husband's retirement she wanted to stay with her son. Even when her daughter-in-law showed definite signs of hostility towards her, she did not want to leave her son and stay separate.

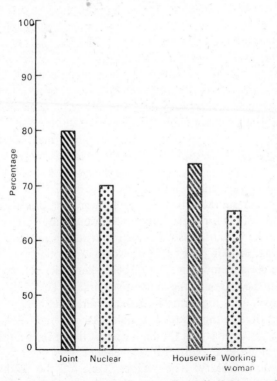

Fig. 19. Percentage of women perferring to live with children in old age, according to type of family and occupational status.

A comparative study was made on the difference in attitude between housewives and working wives on this question. The difference was marginal yet it shows that housewives tend to prefer staying with children more than working wives. Probably housewives become more dependent on husband and children than working wives. Employed wives are more independent economically and hence can plan to be less dependent on children in old age. Whatever the occupational status, over 70% Indian women want to live with their children in old age.

SAVING PATTERNS OF INDIAN WOMEN

Does the average Indian woman believe in saving? Yes, whether it be for difficult days or for her daughter's marriage or for her own old age, she would like to put aside something as saving if she can afford to. When people live a hand-to-mouth existence, the question of saving is difficult. What is earned is spent in their daily expenses. Often when a lifetime is spent repaying loans the question of saving does not arise at all.

Saving is directly related to socio-economic status. While 90% of the urban rich and 78% of the middle class put aside part of their earnings as savings only 27% among the poor are able to save (Fig. 20). The most common feeling expressed by poor women was "when we do not have money to eat our daily meal what have we got to put aside?" Though the desire to save was there, there was no choice since the little money that came in hand was not sufficient for even the daily requirements.

Women among the urban poor, who were completely dependent on their husbands for their daily bread, were quite helpless in this matter. In the labour class men often squander what little they earn in gambling, drinking, or on other women.

Middle class women, in spite of being hard hit, believe in saving because of the standard they have to maintain. They are basically conservative and moderate in their spending habits, and put aside something though their budget is tight. Among the reasons given for a lack of savings was the high cost of living in the cities. Some complained about the numerous dependents they had to support within a fixed salary. The vicious cycle of the high cost of living, increasing need for more and more material comforts, and the limited salary structure, all contributed to a great sense of insecurity in the middle class.

Parvathi, the compounder's wife, spoke with despair, "When I see how well off some people are and our own poor standard, I get disgusted with life. We may not have money to save but we do need money to feed ourselves and our children." The lower economic strata of society wishes to imitate the better off and when they are unable to, there is a growing sense of frustration.

Hierarchy of Saving Patterns

In what would Indian women like to invest? Jewellery, house, bank deposit, business shares, or insurance? Consistently the upper and middle socio-economic strata in all the regions show the same hierarchy of saving patterns. Their first choice is for a house or some land, then bank deposits, jewellery, shares, and lastly insurance.

A place to live was felt by many to be most necessary. If they had a house of their own they would not feel insecure in old age. Many women were acutely conscious of the severe housing problem in Indian cities, and their dream was to have a house of their own preferably in their native town or village.

The strong desire expressed by most women to have a house shows the firm conservatism of the Indian woman. Her first concern is for a home, which is the very nucleus of a stable family life, and which gives her and her family a social standing. In the insecurity of modern times when everything is short-lived and every value changeable, one's own house, however small, gives a sense of belonging. Only the Central region in all the strata was an exception in preferring bank deposits to investment in a house. Bank deposits was the second choice for investment in the higher and middle social strata in all the areas except the Central zone. Women of the low social group especially in the West, North and Central regions said saving in a bank was the best form of investment. Many ayahs and cooks mentioned putting aside a little money in the bank every month, as the most convenient way of investing.

Muniamma, a doctor's ayah, gratefully said, "It was my mistress who helped me to open an account and encouraged me to put some money in the bank every month. Now I have over a thousand rupees. Someday, I hope to have a small shop of my own." Investing in jewellery is less popular among women of all sections in the society. Even women of the low socio-economic strata give only second place to saving in jewellery. The women of the lowest strata of the Eastern region consider investing in jewellery as their third choice, as keeping jewellery safe has become extremely

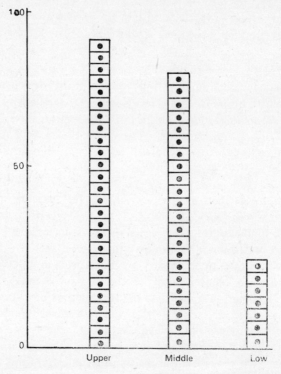

Fig. 20. Percentage of women saving in relation to socio-economic status.

difficult in big cities. Besides, the high cost of gold has made it very difficult for women of the middle and low socio-economic strata to primarily invest in gold and jewellery. Women are convinced that investing in a house or keeping money in the bank is preferable to buying and keeping gold.

Insurance as a mode of saving was least popular among all sections of women all over the country. Many women did not have any precise idea about insurance. Some less educated women thought it was for their husband's office to bother about it and they had nothing to do in the matter. Some felt insurance money was always enjoyed by those left behind after one's death. A few gave definite reasons as to why they would not invest in insurance. They felt the money was not available when needed. Besides, when the family did not have a fixed income, regular payment of insurance premium was difficult. For many women of the higher strata investing in shares appears more practical and useful than insurance. It is unfortunate that so much ignorance exists about the value and necessity for insurance.

Of all the women interviewed, only three mentioned they would like to invest their money on the education of their children which they thought would be the best way to save.

CONSUMER RESPONSIBILITIES

Women were encouraged to discuss their responsibilities in checking the price rise. They were asked what contribution they could make as a consumer to hold the price line.

Though 17 different approaches were mentioned as listed below,

Table 23

DIFFERENT APPROACHING TO RESISTING PRICE LINE

	Socio-economic Class		
	Upper	Middle	Low
Spend minimum	19.20	19.20	21.20
Avoid black market	10.80	5.40	8.80
Buy only essentials	32.00	36.00	12.40
Supplement income	8.40	5.20	28.80
Avoid wastage	4.80	3.60	10.00
Budgeting	3.60	1.60	4.80
Avoid hoarding	2.40	0.60	—
Resist adulteration	1.20	0.20	—
Save	0.80	0.20	1.20
Have only one meal	0.80	0.20	4.00
Resist price rise	2.40	0.80	—
Strike	1.20	0.80	—
Less entertainment	1.60	0.40	0.40
Limit family size	1.60	—	0.40
Buy only from co-operative stores	0.40	1.00	—
Do not have servants	—	0.20	—
Bargaining	—	—	0.40

the first four were most popular. The next two were favoured by some and the rest were suggested by just a few.

Buying only essential items was the most popular approach for the high and middle socio-economic groups, while supplementing the income stood as the most popular way to handle price rise for the poor. The problem with the poor was that they did not have money in hand even to buy essential commodities so the question of limiting purchases to essential items was hypothetical. Many however, felt that they had to spend a minimum of what little they earned as every expense had to be met with their meagre wages. The easiest way out as suggested by many was to work and supplement the family income.

In many middle class families there is a tendency to buy in-essentials to keep up a false sense of status. As Mrs Kulkarni aptly put it, "The greatest curse with us middle class people is that we are neither here nor there. The rich can afford numerous luxuries as they have the money to indulge in vulgar display. The poor have no money and so limit their expense to the basics. Many middle class families have a tendency to go for items more for show and fashion than for actual necessity. We as women can help the family to stop this habit. For instance, at home I always keep some home made snacks so that the children do not get into the habit of buying eats from outside. With regard to clothes I make it a point never to make more than three good dresses for each child. When one is worn out, they have the choice to get a new one in place."

It was surprising that in spite of the tight budget among the middle class, many women did not have any constructive suggestions to offer for checking price rise. The desperate answer given by many was "What can we do? We can just buy what is absolutely essential." This shows their passive role. The high socio-economic group with better status and social involvement expressed their views on consumer responsibilities. However, as the price rise affected them less, they did not show the enthusiasm displayed by the less rich.

POLITICAL INTEREST

Political consciousness is not high in Indian women except among those who are in high positions. However, if they are considered according to socio-economic status, the women of the high strata show greater political interest. Better education, greater social consciousness and awareness about political events draw their attention to politics. They read the papers, keep themselves acquainted with political trends and often discuss politics with friends and family members. 42% of the women in the top category all over the country expressed their interest in politics. The percentage of women showing political interest in the middle socio-economic groups is half that of the upper group, and in the lower group political awareness is less than 10% (Fig. 21). Politics

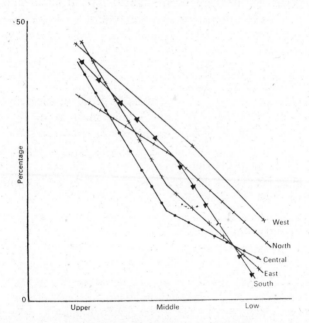

Fig. 21. Percentage of women showing political awareness according to socio-economic status and region.

is a full time business. Its intricacies, tactics and strategies are often too much for the average woman. They have so many other problems to bother about. Politics draws their attention only when major happenings take place like the death of a leader, elections, war, or a natural crisis.

Mrs Madanlal said, "What does it matter as to who rules or which party is in power. They are all the same. What really concerns middle class people like us is that we would like to get at least food and clothing at reasonable prices."

Mrs Phillip, a Ph.D. in philosophy, complained, "Politics has become very unpredictable and too dirty a business. It has nothing to offer a fair-minded, conscientious man or woman. The low level to which modern politics has sunk all over the world is sickening. Don't expect me to waste my time and energy discussing politics."

The better educated women belonging to a high social status though not involved in politics did evince some interest in political matters. Many were aware that a lot depended on political stability in the country. They had some desire to keep themselves informed about what was happening in India and in the world around.

Persons Most Admired

Though Indian women do not profess great political consciousness, the choice of the person they admire most is usually a political leader. Whether it be Gandhi, Nehru, Indira Gandhi, Patel, Subhas Chandra Bose, Lincoln, Kennedy or Golda Myer, the first rank is given to a politician.

The most frequently mentioned names were those of Gandhi and Nehru. As they are now memories of the past, women often elevated these leaders to the position of saints and spoke about them with awe and admiration. They remembered them for the remarkable role they had played as national heroes. Subhas Chandra Bose, Patel, Shastri and Krishna Menon were described as great men who had brought credit to the country. Indira Gandhi was popular with upper class women as the architect of modern India, the one who had elevated the very status of Indian women, and as the most dynamic woman they had ever known.

Some educated women belonging to the younger age group mentioned political personalities other than Indians. This was most evident in college-going girls. A few women belonging to the lower-middle strata mentioned the name of the local M.L.A. or mayor as most admired. This was specially evident in the lower strata in the South and Central zones. Though women of the different socio-economic strata in the East, South and Central regions ranked politicians as the most admired, the economically backward in the North zone stood apart in giving saints a higher status. Most Sikh women ranked saints over politicians.

Whether writers, film stars or saints took a second rank depended on the area and the socio-economic status of the women. The top category women in all the areas except the West gave a second rank to writers. The society women of the West however gave this place to saints. Middle class women do not show a consistency in their choice of the person for the second rank. Each zone had its own specific choice except women of the South and North. Both these groups gave the second place to saints. The women of the lower strata gave the second place to film stars or to some family member depending on the area of origin. The third, fourth and fifth ranks were taken by saints, film stars, writers, poets, musicians or social workers depending on the area of origin and social status. Sri Ramakrishna, Vivekananda, Ramana Maharshi, Saibaba, Satya Saibaba, Dayananda Saraswati, Meerabai, Tulsidas, Guru Nanak, Guru Govind, Radha Swami were some of the religious leaders mentioned by different groups.

The provincial colouring was evident in the choice of film stars, writers, musicians, poets and social workers. Popular film stars mentioned were Dilip Kumar, Meena Kumari, Raj Kapoor, Vyjayantimala, Hema Malini, Dharmendra, Sivaji Ganeshan, Gemini Ganeshan, Prem Nazir, Uttam Kumar, Suchitra Sen etc. In the South and East zones there was a local flavour in their choice of film stars.

Writers mentioned were mainly those belonging to the provincial groups like Sarat Chandra, Mahadevi Varma, Yash Pal and Tendulkar, Bhagvati Charan Verma, Sumitra Nandan Pant and others. As reading habits were often limited to reading of vernacular books this was not surprising. Well known English writers were mentioned mainly by women in college, teachers, and women academicians.

In the choice of musicians, both classical and popular singers were mentioned. Playback singers like Lata, Mohammad Rafi, Kishore, Gantasala, Vani Jayaram, and Jesudas were more popular than classical artists.

South Indian women gave the widest variety in the names mentioned. Then came the East and West and then the North and Central regions. This probably was due to the greater exposure and involvement of women in artistic and cultural activities in certain states than in others.

RELIGION

People in India are in general very religious although many do not have any organised form of worship. Whether young or old, poor or rich, the Indian woman is basically religious. Religious concepts and attitudes differ among the young and old. Over 90% of the women in this study expressed that they assign an important role to religion in every day life. They consider it necessary for a fuller and happier life.

Table 24

BELIEF IN RELIGION IN DIFFERENT AGE GROUPS

Response	Age group									
	15-24		25-34		35-44		More than 45		Total	
	No.	%	No.	%	No.	%	No.	%	No.	%
No	21	9.56	32	8.20	16	6.06	4	3.50	73	7.30
Yes	210	90.44	358	91.80	248	93.94	111	96.50	927	92.70
Total	231	100.00	390	100.00	264	100.00	115	100.00	1000	100.00

Meenakshi, a second year college student, said that she did think of God and felt drawn to the concept which was however very different from her parent's idea of religion. Her parents attended "satsang" every week, arranged prayer meetings, and discourses in their home. "I am passively drawn to religion and I have made no effort to stop my interest," admitted the young collegian.

Mrs Kapur had this to say, "It gives me great mental peace to believe in God. I have been able to bear so much in life because of my devout nature." Religion is considered an anchor to hold on to by many people especially in times of trouble. Some believe in fasts and going to temples dutifully. Some visit holy places regularly. For many, religion is a part of their daily living. They do not have to make an effort to be pious. Even young people are not shy to admit that they are religious. But they have less time for rituals than the old because of preoccupation with studies and other related activities. Some feel that "there is yet time to get more religious", as Lata put it. "I think religion is for my parents. Maybe when I get older, I will be like them." Among those not religious, Smriti said, "I am an atheist. I hardly think of anything other than what I do." One of the employed women remarked, "Religion retards progress. It is not scientific. It cannot explain or prove many things in life."

On the other hand, for the firm believer, religion nurtures and gives strength to human beings. They accept happiness and sorrow as part of life and are able to bear trials and tribulations with greater fortitude. There is a lesser use of tranquillisers among the religious which proves that inner strength and confidence are attained by virtue of their faith.

Religion is apparently practised by going to places of worship, praying at home quietly, observing fasts, keeping a shrine at home, visiting holy places etc. Since Christians have organised worship in churches, they do go to places of worship regularly. Some Hindus believe in going to a nearby temple every day. To whichever religion a woman belonged, only about 9% of the sample did not go to places of worship. Women educated only up to the middle or high school level were more inclined to visit places of worship.

Hindus, Christians and Sikhs go to places of worship mostly. A large percentage of Muslim women do not visit places of worship as most Muslim shrines do not allow women. Over a third of the Sikhs and Christians go to the gurudwara or church respectively at least once a week. The Hindus are not bound to visit a temple as a mark of piety, and most of them have a shrine at home. It could be anything from a few calendar pictures of their favourite dieties to a miniature temple where elaborate daily worship is done. Most believe in offering prayers at the shrine in their homes. Occasionally they visit temples and observe fasts.

Table 25

RELIGIOUS GROUPS AND THE PRACTISE OF FASTING

	Hindus		Christians		Muslims		Sikhs		Total	
	No.	%	No.	%	No.	%	No.	%	No.	%
Never	261	31.94	26	38.81	21	29.58	27	60.00	335	33.50
Sometimes	467	57.17	41	61.19	48	67.60	15	33.33	571	57.10
Always	89	10.89	—	—	2	2.82	3	6.67	94	9.40
Total	817	100.00	67	100.00	71	100.00	45	100.00	1000	100.00

All denominations oberve fasts to some extent (Table 25). Hindu women observe fasts in accordance with their religious practices. Most Muslims mentioned fasting at least once a year during "roza". Christians observe Lent during the period before Good Friday. Religious rituals are losing hold, especially over the Hindus, and they are willing to adapt their practices to urban life. Modern women fast to get a good husband, a child, or for the cure of diseases etc. Some people fast to reduce weight. Women from a low socio-economic status are often compelled to fast as they do not have enough food.

Most religious orders have spiritual men in whom the people trust, to serve as mediators between God and man. Mostly Hindus and Sikhs believe in spiritual gurus. Only a small percentage of Muslims and Christians accept the importance of a spiritual guide. In the total sample over 33% women gave great significance to the role of spiritual guides.

SOCIAL SERVICE

In social service one could include membership in service clubs, active participation in social work for the uplift of the poor, the incapacitated, orphans, the aged and disabled, collection of funds for the needy etc. Such activities give a sense of dedication and involvement in work for the welfare of society.

How interested is the Indian woman in social work? There was found to be a direct relationship in the educational level of a woman and her socio-economic status. As education increases one becomes more aware of social evils and the plight of fellow human beings, which creates a desire to do something to ameliorate social evils. If one belongs to the upper classes there are greater opportunities, as these women have more leisure and domestic help.

The typical housewife in the middle or lower socio-economic level, though educated, is over burdened with household chores. If she is employed she has very little time even to spare for her family, with the result there is no desire in her to do social service outside the house.

Mrs Mahapatra remarked, "The greatest social service I can do is to my family. I have three young children and an overworked husband. We cannot afford a cook or an ayah. I have only a part-time maid to help me with the washing and cleaning. My husband is busy at the factory from morning till evening. Where do I have the time to go about doing social service. I am more than happy doing my duty to the family."

However, some women even from the middle strata showed great concern about society. Madhuri, the shop keeper's wife, asserted, "One does not have to be rich to do something good. I have studied only up to class V nor are we rich. I do try to help in my own way, like whenever someone in my neighbourhood is in need I go to assist. I spoke to a lady I knew and got admission for an orphan child in a missionary school. When someone known to me is ill, I try to get a doctor for them. With the sewing machine I have, I am teaching a few girls to sew. My husband does not want me to go out and undertake any service. But whenever I get a chance to help others I do it."

For women of the higher social strata to belong to a service club or social service organisation gives them the feeling that they are involved in active social service. The clubs organise projects and give an opportunity to the members to do their best for the community. On the other hand, for the middle or lower class women there are no organised forms of social service activities avilable. Very often the families in a community mutually help each other without even being aware that they are doing "social service". On the other hand, elitist women make a lot of noise about the good work they are doing, and they are aided by publicity in the media.

Ninety-two per cent of educated women in the upper classes claim to make a contribution through social service against 85% in the middle strata with the same level of education. Even if the awareness for community service is there, women cannot be actively drawn into social service unless opportunities are available. Unemployed, educated women form a large bulk in all stratas of society but especially in the middle level. Social awareness should not only be created but opportunities must be provided and specific plans offered to improve the lot of the community. A woman with basic education from the middle or low social strata can help to pass on ideas about family planning, hygiene and child care. Women of a higher strata must discard their patronising attitude and help the less privileged to generate ideas and help themselves. This will carry the message home better. A woman with painted lips and manicured nails may go and lecture on family planning or baby care. The message has no meaning for the women living in chawls or bustees. On the other hand the educated bustee women must be helped to organise for themselves social service projects. This will surely carry the message more effectively.

The majority of Indian women do not have any clearly planned-out mode of spending leisure time. They either follow their husband's interests or just remain preoccupied with house work. Very few properly utilise leisure in healthy recreational activities. Even women of the higher socio-economic level who have servants and plenty of leisure tend to passively accept any form of entertainment without giving any serious thought to the question of re-creation.

The most common type of entertainment for women of all sections is seeing a movie with the family or with friends. However, in the East and Central groups fewer women of the lower socio-economic strata visit cinemas. In the low socio-economic level, cinema is the only amusement most women know of. Very few from this group see a play, attend a music concert, or watch a dance recital. The Southern region, however, has the maximum number of women of the lower strata who get a chance to see a play or a dance.

Some women of the lower strata mentioned that they get a chance to see a play or hear a music recital on festive occasions, when functions are organised in their neighbourhood. The artists are usually amateurs from the same community.

The poor are completely preoccupied in eking out a living, and the question of recreational activities hardly comes in. Manju the maid servant said, "Where do we get the time or the money to go out for fun. I leave the house at seven in the morning and get back at seven in the evening. Even on Sundays I work. Very rarely, on a day off, I go with my friends to the cinema." Some women of the lower strata mentioned going to a temple festival, a church fete, or mela, the only outings they knew of.

Middle-class woman also consider cinema their favourite entertainment. There is more or less the same distribution in all the areas. Theatre is the second preference among middle-class women of the Western and Eastern regions, while those of the South and Central zones prefer music recitals to theatre. North Indian middle-class women find parties more entertaining than concerts, plays or dance recitals, to which, perhaps, they are not sufficiently exposed. Dance programmes are not a popular form of entertainment among the middle class.

The middle class in the North and West zones are fairly fond of parties, while in the East and Central regions they are less enthusiastic. The South group is least interested.

Many middle class women, especially from the South, West and Central regions, mentioned they belonged to music clubs or fine arts associations. Membership to these cultural "sabhas" is as popular among the middle class as club membership is for high society people.

Some middle class women mentioned going to the market with friends or with the husband as a favourite pastime. If they went for marketing in the evening with their husband on the way back they dropped in at a friend's or visited the temple. Mrs Singh, a radio mechanic's wife, said that all the entertainment she had was going for walks with her husband and children on holidays.

Some women of the older age group mentioned attending religious discourses, "satsang" groups, or hearing "bhajans" as their favourite pastime. A few said sitting and listening to the radio was their best recreation. "Katha-kalashepam" was considered the best entertainment by a few middle class women in the West and South regions.

The cinema is the most popular entertainment in the high socio-economic strata. Women of the East and Central region prefer seeing a movie to any other form of entertainment. Parties are a favourite pastime for high society women of all areas except the South, where music takes precedence over parties.

Among upper-class women of all areas except the South, the order of preference is cinema, parties, music recitals, theatre and dance. Only in the South the order is changed to cinema, music concerts, dance, drama and parties. The upper strata of the Southern region did not relish entertaining or being entertained.

Recreation through Sports

Most outdoor sports are good for the health and provide good entertainment. Very few Indian women show any interest in sports. Even among the educated women of the upper socio-economic strata, sports did not mean much. They talked about sport, listened to commentaries and even witnessed matches but rarely played games. Those who played games in school or college usually gave it up after marriage.

Mrs Amarjeeth Singh was a good hockey player throughout school and college, but after marriage she has not touched the bat, because she had no time or opportunity ever since she left college. Even young women just out of school or college mentioned they played no games regularly. Some women said they did play long ago but that was only out of compulsion, as games were compulsory in school. They had no particular aptitude for sports. What little interest they had was lost after their studies. Some women who had done well in sports in college said no facilities for sports were available. The fact of being women decreased their interest in games, as they felt sports was primarily a man's pursuit.

Mrs Mallick complained, "I was a good basket ball player in college but now that I am married and have two kids, my husband will not appreciate it if I go for basket ball practice every other day to some place. I cannot dream of achieving the impossible. Women, unlike men, have to forego certain things when they marry and become mothers."

Most upper class women in spite of having the opportunity, prefer to adopt a passive attitude to sports. When a wife acccompanies her husband to the club, she has a cold drink or chats while her husband plays tennis or squash. Women are usually bystanders since most of them have never had any consistent opportunity to participate in sports. However, those who played in college often retain their fondness for outdoor games more than professional women, probably because the latter are too preoccupied with their career. The less educated fall into a conservative pattern of society and hence do not maintain their interests after finishing school.

Women of the backward sections hardly play any outdoor games. In the present study, only one woman out of three with college level education said she played badminton. Badminton was the most commonly mentioned outdoor game played by women. Other popular games were tennis, basket ball and hockey respectively. Surprisingly, not even one woman said she played cricket. Some mentioned swimming as a favourite pastime.

Indoor games are popular with all categories of women. To unmarried young women indoor games played with relatives or friends provides leisure. Carom, ludo, snakes and ladders, cards, chess, and scrabble are some indoor games mentioned by women of the middle and higher strata. Women of the lower strata mentioned Indian games played with pebbles, shells, or tamarind seeds, "chaturang", and snakes and ladders. For the rich, cards is the favourite pastime. Mrs Arora proudly said that four hours of card playing with friends every day fetches sufficient money to buy sarees and cosmetics every month. Tambola is popular specially with those who go for ladies' committee parties. A few mentioned doing yoga in place of games as a form of relaxation.

As there is a dearth of space in urban areas, one has to arrange for group activities not absolutely restricted to the home. With the joint family system gradually disappearing less restrictions are imposed on women's social activities. On the whole 39% of women have social outings often and 48% occasionally and the rest never have outings. Having outings depends on numerous factors like money, availability of time, convenience at home, and the willingness and opportunities to go places.

Recreation and Reading Habits

The reading habits of Indian women are directly related to education and to some extent to their socio-economic status. Over 80% of Indian women with primary school education never read. When the education increases to the middle/high school level the reading habit dramatically shows an improvement. Even in the lower socio-economic strata where only about 8% read magazines with primary school education, the percentage increases to over 41% with middle/high school level. The habit of reading the newspaper also improves from 3% to 24%. Once education improves, whatever the status, women are keen to be better informed.

Sujata Bhasin claimed she read more than her husband. "We get four different magazines and two dailies. My husband, who is in business and has late working hours, hardly gets time to read even the morning newspaper. I am the one to give him all the news each day. After sending my daughters to college and my husband to work I read the daily paper and the magazines thoroughly. This has become a daily habit."

The socio-economic strata decides the opportunities a woman gets to read books and magazines. A typical educated housewife from the middle and low socio-economic strata has fewer oppor-

tunities to buy books and magazines or go to libraries or recreational clubs with library facilities. Some educated women of the
middle socio-economic strata said that as they did not get the daily
newspaper at home it was not possible to know the daily news. It
was, however, easier for them to read books and magazines which
they borrowed from neighbours or friends. Even among women
of the high socio-economic strata, magazine reading is more popular than the newspaper.

Mrs Jamal, a full-time housewife who is a graduate, explained,
"We are more concerned with entertainment, cinema and fashion
than about politics. I hardly glance through the headlines of the
morning paper but I read cover to cover of at least two leading
women's magazines."

Mrs Shastri, an M. Sc. in chemistry, felt on the other hand that
women lagged behind men because they were concerned far too
much about frivolous things like fashion and romantic short stories
than about world events and happenings in the country. While
professional women are more particular about reading the daily
paper, college level educated women show a preference for
magazines.

The habit of reading books is closely related to the socio-economic level of the women. The higher the strata and better the educational level, the more is a woman interested in becoming
knowledgeable. She has greater opportunities to buy or borrow
books and discovers the joy of relaxation through reading.

Nearly 75% women in the lower socio-economic level in the
East, North and Central regions never read books, while the West
and South show a slightly better picture with 70% and 68% respectively who do not read books. Even in the middle socio-economic
strata, West and South stand apart from the other regions for the
fact that women show a greater interest in reading. In the higher
class there is no marked difference areawise. In the entire sample
over 30% of women do not read at all.

The type of books women read has relation not only to the
socio-economic status but also to the area of origin to some extent.
Novels are most popular in the higher and middle groups. Fiction
is usually more favoured than religious and educational books
because even women with a light reading taste are satisfied by
them. Educational books take second place among women in the
higher and middle strata. Only the middle class South Indian group

shows a preference for religious books over educational ones. More women from the Western region read educational books as compared to other areas. The North zone upper class women top the list for reading novels, then the Eastern and Central areas respectively. The West and South show the same picture in their preference for novels to other types of books.

In the middle socio-economic group, women in the West are most fond of novels, then comes the Northern group. The East and Central regions reveal a similar picture while the Southern middle strata lags behind in their interest for fiction.

When we take the lower socio-economic status, the East, North and Central regions show a preference for religious books to novels and educational books. While in the West and South, the preference is for novels over religious books. It is not uncommon to see a woman with just primary school education reading the *Ramayana*, *Mahabharata* or *Geeta*. With the educational level improving, a woman's interest extends to a variety of subjects.

If women are to play a more important role in society they have to widen their interests. It is indeed discouraging to note that even among the upper socio-economic strata, only 50% are interested in educational books while over 75% read novels. Though reading is often done as a casual means of recreation or even to kill time, the reading habit should be more fruitfully cultivated in order to widen one's knowledge of oneself and one's environment.

SIX

Fashion

The prevailing fashion, particularly in dress, is followed as rigidly as a custom. Every age has standards of dress and personal grooming in keeping with the times. Fashion is created by a few for the majority to follow. When new trends set in, the old is set aside until still newer trends make the existing fashions outdated.

The fashions of the Victorian age, when women were dressed in frills and laces from neck to ankle would appear outlandish to the twentieth century person. The fashions of the modern age when women wear more to show than to cover up would have seemed indecent and vulgar even fifty years ago.

Every country has its native flavour in fashion. What an African woman would consider fashionable whether it be rings to elongate her neck or tattoo to cover her back would look primitive to a western woman. The Indian woman's apparent lack of shame in exposing her midriff while she covers her face in a "ghoonghat" would tickle a conservative New Englander. Fashion thus has diversity, variety and mobility.

However, the modern concept of fashion has a new dimension added to it, that is uniformity. There is a great desire in every part of the world to fall in line with a pattern set in affluent America or Paris at the expense of its own indigenous variety. This desire to import fashion cults from outside corrodes the traditional values of one's country and social group.

Mass media through press, cinema, and advertisement helps build up a 'fashion hysteria'. With the idea of introducing novelty in clothes and styles, it projects imported fashions as the most fabulous and sophisticated. Many belonging to the higher socio-economic group especially those of the younger age discard their own cultural patterns as outdated and take to imported styles without any consideration of taste or suitability.

In an old, fairly conservative society one expects changes in fashion to come about slowly. There is a reluctance to accept the new. Among the factors influencing fashion, the most important is people's eagerness for variety.

How eager is the Indian woman to follow fashion? Where does she get her ideas on fashion? What is the prevailing mode of dress and what is her choice? Has she conditioned herself to accepting mod clothes?

The last century has seen a rapid change in men's clothes and hair styles in every part of India. In an urban population to see men with a luxuriant tuft on the scalp or glistening earrings is more an exception than a rule. The Indian male's mode of dress is by and large western except for those living in rural areas or in cases where an effort is made to keep the native flavour in dress by wearing a "dhoti", "churidar" or a turban. The Indian woman on the other hand is exceptionally firm in her convictions on dress and style. She is more indigenous in her dress than the male.

Fashion trends are set by the few in the upper classes who long for novelty and change, or for creating a particular effect. Being in a prestigious position in society they can flout the prevailing trends and start something new, which is then promptly followed by others. The followers get the feeling that they are being more sophisticated and their ego is satisfied.

FASHION CONSCIOUSNESS

How aware is the Indian woman about fashions and how eager is she to follow them? Around 10% of the sample are very conscious of fashions and nearly 30% not at all. In the higher strata of society more than 17% consider themselves fashionable and over 70% are moderately interested. Only a few look upon themselves as completely lacking fashion sense.

As we go down the socio-economic scale, we find a definite trend towards conservatism. Nearly 30% of the middle socio-economic strata and 60% of the lower strata are absolutely indifferent to fashion. Only 10% of the middle group and 3% of the lower classes claim they are very fashion conscious (Fig. 22).

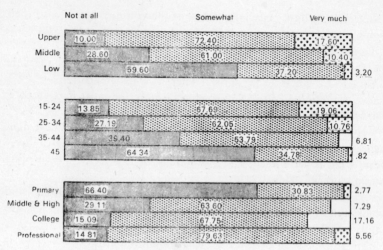

Fig. 22. Fashion consciousness in relation to socio-economic status, age, and educational level.

Vimla, a sweeper in Lucknow, wore silver "kadas" and a "choker" on her neck. ' All my people have dressed the way I do. As far as I know, my grandmother, my aunts, and mother have worn a saree and a blouse and the type of jewellery I am wearing. What is the need for a change? I am happy the way I am."

It is encouraging to note that about 60% of the middle socio-economic group and slightly less than 40% of the lower strata feel they are moderately fashion conscious and want to look attractive and follow the example set by others. The average woman is prevented from being over concerned with fashion as she is pre-occupied with domestic chores, and cannot be over bothered about clothes and personal appearance. Money, greater exposure to fashion trends, leisure, and lack of inhibitions make it easy for women of the higher strata to follow fashions.

The idea that a certain restraint is expected of a family woman is deep rooted. Once her children reach the teenage level, she is more concerned with the appearance of her daughters than herself. She may keep herself clean, wear good clothes but not with the idea of parading herself.

Mrs Panigrahi, a middle aged Oriya lady with three children, scoffed at the idea of fashion. "It is for cinema stars and dancers, not for housewives," she asserted. "Why do I have to bother about fashions with my hair starting to grey. Even my two daughters are like me. We wear good clothes and keep clean but not for impressing others." There is a certain mental maturity in Indian women which makes nearly 90% refrain from indulging madly in fashion.

The Younger Woman and Fashion

Women belonging to the younger age group are definitely more fashion-conscious as they feel a greater desire for recognition. They come across new trends and are willing to follow them. With increasing age, there is a proportionate decrease in fashion awareness. Even among the young there is a conservative tendency which makes approximately two-thirds of them moderate in their tastes. Slightly over 10% declare that they are not fashionable at all. The proportion is much less in comparison to 40% of the middle aged and about 65% of elderly women who are not at all fashion-oriented (Fig. 22). However, the entire lot of young women have not been drawn into the new wave in fashions, the reason being conservative upbringing, family tradition, and lack of opportunity and purchasing power.

Miss Vinita, a third year student in college, felt that to be progressive was to be with the times. One must follow fashion if one has to make any headway in life. Fashion gives a woman certain poise and confidence that she will be recognized and accepted. She felt that most girls in her class were old fashioned and outdated, because they were scared to go against convention.

Miss Champa, an Andhra girl working as a stenotypist, felt that fashion was more for the rich and not for middle class girls like herself. "Fashion is not essential to be successful in life. Women who have the money and leisure waste their time and money on the latest designs in clothes and hair styles even though they might look vulgar and cheep and not dignified," she added. The idea of looking mod by parading in ultra modern clothes and hair styles is a comparatively new trend derived from the West. In many parts of India, especially in the Punjab, U.P., and Rajasthan, an unmarried girl is not allowed to wear very flashy clothes or jewellery. Simplicity is the general rule. Only after marriage does she get the licence to use cosmetics, jewels and fashionable clothes. This pattern is however changing in affluent urban families.

Fashion and Education

Fashion consciousness increases with education. Two-thirds among the illiterate or educated upto primary school are not particular about fashions. Among the middle and high school group only about 30% are not fashion conscious while the figure drops to 15% in those with college education and among the professionally qualified. When women are educated, there is an increased awareness towards fashion. There is greater exposure and desire to follow new trends as a sign of being progressive. However, among the professionally qualified women like doctors, lawyers, research workers and scientists, there is a lesser desire to be very fashionable. These women have other preoccupations, and do not have either the time or patience to be fashion-conscious. Wasting time on fashions appears to be frivolous to a professional woman.

Mrs Samuel, a professor of physics, has put it aptly: "Whoever has the time to keep up with fashion trends when there are many more worthwhile things to do. After all, with education one's sense of values change and fashion takes a secondary place to other interests and pursuits."

Nevertheless a professional woman has a very special place in society. She knows she cannot afford to be shabbily dressed and outdated. About 80% of the professionals assert they are moderate in their clothe styles. Their prime concern is convenience and simplicity.

For the majority of Indian women, educated or illiterate, the idea of being a sex object is repulsive. This may be the reason why they disapprove fashions which emphasise sex. The notion that women must be fashionable to win a man or to impress others is an imported idea. Even education has not achieved much in bringing about a complete change in women's attitudes to fashion.

Fashion and Region

The idea of fashion varies greatly from area to area. Even for a fashionable Malayali, lipstick may not be a necessary item. It may be an artistically put sandle paste "tilak" on the forehead or hair loosely braided to cover her ears. For a Tamilian it may be more fashionable to wear golden "jhumkas" and don flowers in the hair than walk in slacks like a man. For a woman in U.P., a fashionable style mny mean matching glass bangles or attractive earrings. Native fashions in India have much variety and diversity.

Table 26

CHOICE OF DRESS ACCORDING TO SOCIO-ECONOMIC STATUS

| Dress | Socio-economic status | | | | | | | |
| | Upper | | Middle | | Low | | Total | |
	No.	%	No.	%	No.	%	No.	%
Saree	218	87.20	457	91.40	219	87.60	894	89.40
Other	32	12.80	43	8.60	31	12.40	106	10.60
Total	250	100.00	500	100.00	250	100.00	1000	100.00

Table 27

CHOICE OF DRESS ACCORDING TO DIFFERENT REGIONS

| Choice Dress | Regions | | | | | | | | | | | |
| | East | | West | | South | | North | | Central | | Total | |
	No.	%	No.	%	No.	%	No.	%	No	%	No.	%
Saree	186	93.00	175	87.50	188	94.00	154	77.00	191	95.50	894	89.40
Other	14	7.00	25	12.50	12	6.00	46	23.00	9	4.50	106	10.60
Total	200	100.00	200	100.00	200	100.00	200	100.00	200	100.00	1000	100.00

Western trends projected through magazines and films are more uniform in all areas. With education and an improved social standing, tastes tend to be more uniform. Indigenous habits are shed and new ones are adopted.

The great majority mention the saree as the dress of their choice. Even an improved socio-economic status makes no significant difference. The middle socio-economic group being slightly more conservative, over 90% opt for the saree. Women prefer the saree since it is elegant and most comfortable. The average woman's question was—"What is the need to take to a new mode of dress when the saree is so graceful and never gets outdated?"

In the higher socio-economic strata 12% prefer slacks, pants, salwar kameez or maxis. An equal proportion in the lower socio-economic strata also prefer other modes of dress to the saree. These women opt for their own regional dress like the Malayalis' choice of the mundu, the Punjabi Sikh's salwar kameez, and the Gujarati's or Rajasthani's "gharara."

When we consider the dress of choice according to area of origin, we find the women of the East, South and Central regions more traditional in their dress, the most conservative being the Central region. The West and North are more progressive in their choice of dress with North giving the greatest priority to variety in dress. Twenty three per cent women from the North prefer some other dress to the saree (Table 27), one of the main reasons being that the North has been subjected to more foreign influences than the rest of India.

The West with Bombay as the nucleus has been the centre of fashion. Women are more exposed to new trends and readily adapt different modes of dressing. This city has the largest number of working girls. Consequently more women enjoy greater economic freedom to try the latest fashion. The South and East, being more traditional, are less willing to accept new fashions in dress. Central India again shows a conservative picture in the attitude to dress. It is less influenced by the North or West. Uttar Pradesh being the stronghold of Hindustani culture is least prepared to give up the saree as the dress of the choice.

Excluding the saree and one's own community dress, slacks and shirt seemed most popular among Indian women wanting a change.

Unconventional Dress

It is encouraging to note that over 46% women belonging to the higher and middle socio-economic strata are not prejudiced against the occasional use of unconventional clothes. About 35% women of the top category favour regular wearing of unconventional dress. When it comes to the use of such clothes frequently the women of the middle socio-economic strata show a sudden drop to less than 20%. However, nearly half the women belonging to the middle strata do not mind other women wearing unconventional clothes.

Even two decades ago it was very unbecoming of a Punjabi girl to move around without a "dupatta" or for a South Indian girl to go without a "dawani". Now many girls move in pants and shirt or a maxi and the family raises no objection. It is the same even in a conservative Marwari home or a traditional Bengali family where girls used to wear sarees before puberty. Now girls move about in other styles of clothing often very untraditional and 'mod.' They are now openly accepted in an urban society. Even older women, especially from the upper strata from all states of India wear unconventional clothes on holidays, during travel, picnics, or parties. This is accepted as part of modern living.

The women of the lower strata are very conservative about even occasionally wearing unconventional clothes. The gap in education and income being very wide between the higher and the lower group, habits and attitudes of the higher strata are not easily accepted and adopted by a lower socio-economic group. The middle class is more easily falling in line with the higher socio-economic group at least in their attitudes if not in actual practice.

The attitude to dress is also related to the educational level. With better education women become broad-minded. From about 15% among the middle and high school educated women the favourableness increases to 30% in the group educated upto the college level and 35% among the professional women. In the overall sample less than one-fifth approve of unconventional dresses.

Mamata, a Bengali jute worker's wife, did not approve of women in 'mod' clothes. "We dress to cover ourselves. If we want to expose our body why wear clothes at all?"

Vijayalakshmi, a postal clerk's wife, also looked down on fashionable clothes. "We look best in a saree", she said. "For a small child a frock or any other dress is alright. After a girl attains puberty it is necessary that she dress with modesty."

Mrs Pai, an insurance agent, felt a woman's dress reveals a lot about her character. "The first step to losing one's character is to discard conservative clothes and adopt western ones," she emphasised.

The factors that have helped popularise unconventional clothes are films, woman's magazines, and advertisements, as the higher strata of society readily accept these as trend setters. The middle and lower group emulate women of the higher strata. Women of lesser social standing feel they will be better recognised in society if they accept the norms of the socially well-placed. This often frustrates the underprivileged as they cannot live like the higher classes. The conservative level of society to which they belong discards them as misfits.

Mrs Mitra, the principal of a Bengali girls' high school, is very correct when she says, "The fashion trends set by most women's magazines and the movies are incompatible with Indian women's tastes and sensibilities. They cause frustration for an average young woman who is unable to live up to those new levels of style projected through magazines and movies. They do more harm than benefit to women."

Lipstick

The use of lipstick is a borrowed fashion habit. Though even in ancient India there were methods of colouring the lips with beetle juice or herbal dyes for increasing one's attractiveness lipstick as such is typically western. The popularity of lipstick with Indian women decreases from the higher to the lower socio-economic strata. The percentage drops to half from around 32% of regular lipstick users in the higher level to 16% in the middle socio-economic group. The use of lipstick in the lower strata is negligible, with only a little over 1% using this cosmetic regularly.

Though nearly 80% of the lower strata have not accepted the use of lipstick, around 20% do not mind using it occasionally. This shows that the use of lipstick, though definitely determined by the socio-economic level, has gained popularity even among the lower strata.

In considering the popularity of lipstick among women of different areas, we find that the use of lipstick is predominantly a phenomenon among women of the North belonging to the higher socio-economic strata of society. Over 62% of these women use it regularly. The Central region with U.P. near Delhi is catching up with the North by having 52% lipstick users. The East, with 26%, is between the progressive and conservative. The West and South have only 14% and 10% respectively of regular lipstick-users. Women from the South seem to be the most conservative group in this respect.

Even among the fashion-conscious women of the middle class the use of lipstick has not become very popular. However, it is worth noting how a typical western style of cosmetic has caught up in all regions among the higher classes. Only the Southern region is trailing behind. In an urban population, conservative practices change with intermixture of ideas from other regions and groups. An average individual wants to fall in with the 'progressive' higher class in their views be it on social change, fashion, eating habits, flower arrangement or family planning.

Though the women of the lower strata in society are less educated and more conservative, their ideal is to toe the line of fashion set by the higher social classes. Among the various restraining factors in the lower strata, the low economic condition in which they live is significant. Among the urban poor one would only occasionally see a woman in hipster saree or gaudy costume jewellery or bright lipstick in imitation of the newly rich. Fortunately this is not a mass transformatian due to poor economic conditions, lack of educational opportunities, and what is most important, the traditional tag of conservatism which the Indian woman still carries.

IDEAS OF FASHION

From where does the Indian woman gather her ideas about fashion? Nearly half the women who were surveyed said they got their ideas from friends or by observing neighbours or others. They said they did not bother to look into books or magazines for the latest trends. In all the areas the answer was consistent and the figures more or less tallied to about 50%, except in the Southern group which showed a slightly higher figure of 57% (Table 29).

Magazines were next in importance as fashion setters. Nearly

25% are influenced by ideas presented mostly through women's magazines. In the Central region alone the percentage is 17%.

Table 28

SOURCES OF FASHION IN RELATION TO SOCIO-ECONOMIC STATUS

Sources	Socio-economic status		
	Upper	Middle	Low
Magazines	42.40	23.20	4.80
Films	13.60	12.20	7.60
Friends	54.40	56.20	36.80
Own	26.80	8.20	1.60
Not applicable	9.60	25.20	54.50

Table 29

SOURCES OF FASHION IN RELATION TO REGION

Sources	East	West	South	North	Central
Magazine	25.00	24.50	23.60	27.00	17.00
Films	12.00	10.50	20.50	7.50	7.50
Friends	49.50	48.50	57.00	49.00	50.50
Own	12.00	7.50	10.00	14.50	12.00

Over 42% of higher society women look to women's magazines for fashions compared to only 23% women of the middle class. It may be because they have less opportunity to buy magazines. Hence they are unable to follow fashion trends regularly from these magazines. Besides, the styles projected through magazines may have less appeal due to their conservative background.

Only a very small percentage of 10 to 14% use their imagination and originality in dressing. When we consider the different socio-economic groups, we find a significant change only in the higher strata of society, where the number of women who use their originality increases. While over 25% women of the higher socio-economic strata have ideas of their own, only 8% of women in the middle level group use imagination in dressing.

Films occupy the lowest factor as an influence on women regarding fashion trends. It is interesting to note that 8% women of the lower socio-economic strata are influenced by films. Films have definitely been a convenient media for propagating latest fashion trends to the lower sections of society though more often the fashion projected is unsuitable for the average women. South Indian women are more influenced by films than women from other areas. The reason may be that South Indian films are more indigenous in taste and cater to local flavour in style.

On an average nearly 33% of Indian women belonging to all areas do not go out of their way to acquire ideas on fashion trends. They dress for convenience and necessity and are not very conscious of fashion trends. When we consider the socio-economic factor more than half of the lower strata have no desire to follow the new wave in fashion. The middle level of about 25% bridges the gap between 10% in the higher strata of women and 54% in the lower strata.

Fashion consciousness exists mainly among young, college going women and those of the higher strata. The majority of Indian women are only moderately fashion conscious, and stick to the saree as the ideal mode of dress. They use lipstick seldom and gather their ideas of fashion primarily from friends and relatives. The fashion hysteria of the affluent industrialised countries of the West is yet to overtake our women. Sobriety in taste and habits, her traditional and cultural background, and poverty have all contributed to check a mass transformation of the Indian woman.

SMOKING

In the entire sample only about one-third of the women approve of smoking. In this attitude working wives are liberal and housewives conservative. Conservative women consider smoking a vice and a hazard to health.

When the question is considered regionwise the East and North upper socio-economic groups are most liberal, and over 60% of the top category women in both these groups approve smoking. Then come the high society women in the South Indian group and middle class women of the East. The middle level is consistently conservative with 72% not in favour. Only in the East is the attitude more liberal. In all the areas in the lowest lot except the West and Central regions only around one-third of the women approve smoking.

Do women smoke in this country? In general Indian women are

not smokers. The highest percentage of smokers are in the top category East and North regions which is around 20%. The high society women of the Central region come next with 18% smokers. The women of the West and South even in the higher socio-economic strata are least habituated to smoking. Middle class women are uniformly conservative in all areas with a negligible number smoking in the East and Western regions. The poorer classes also show a conservative picture with 8% women smokers.

Village women occasionally smoke "tamaku", "bidi" or "churat", but when they migrate cities they imitate socially better placed urban women. They begin to feel some of their rural habits such as wearing no blouse, wearing big nose-rings or smoking "tamaku", are *infra dig*. They get rid of these habits to fit into what they believe a more civilized, cultured pattern of life. Deepurani, a Bengali living in Calcutta said, "In *desh* many elderly women smoke 'tamaku'. But in Calcutta we do not smoke as we will be looked down upon as vulgar." Among the poor their not smoking raises them to a better status, as in caste socialisation it is usually seen that the lower caste imitates the higher caste for elevating its status.

Drinking

Drinking is not a new phenomenon in any society. In the past

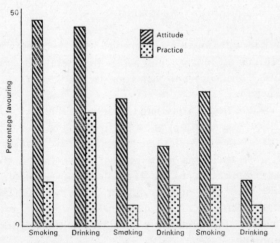

Fig. 23. Attitude towards smoking and drinking.

people drank toddy and other native brews believed to relax the nerves and have nutritious value. Now with the advance of technology, more sophisticated drinks are available which are taken especially by the elite.

Generally speaking Indian women neither drink nor approve of drinking because of their conservative background. Mostly women in the upper socio-economic strata approve of drinking; nearly half of them have no objection. The percentage drops to less than 20% in the middle strata and to about 10% in the lower group. In the lower socio-economic group, drinking is neither a sign of affluence nor status. The usual complaint by women is that their husbands waste money on liquor when they do not have enough to feed themselves. Many marriages are wrecked because of excessive drinking by husbands. When considered areawise, the highest approval of drinking is in the North and the least from the Central region. On the whole less than one-fourth of the sample approved drinking.

The tolerance of wives of their husbands' drinking has relation to whether they themselves drink or not. If they drink, the approval rate is doubled (Fig. 24). Over 25% of the women in the upper socio-economic strata drink, against 9% in the middle and 5% in the lowest strata. For upper class women drinking is a matter of fashion. Because of the popularity of social drinking among the

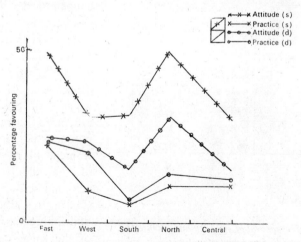

Fig. 24. Attitude towards smoking (s) and drinking (d) and practice of smoking and drinking regionwise.

urban rich, women not only approve of drinking but often drink in company. Mrs Bhatra put it, "I cannot help drinking. My husband is a company executive and we often attend social get-togethers where most men and women drink." This was the excuse of many women of the upper socio-economic strata. If the husband drinks he encourages his wife to, so that she tolerates the circle in which they move. Mrs Sumani admitted, "I do not really care for drinks, but I take a little for my husband's sake. I would be bored to death in parties where my husband takes me if I sat there with just a glass of tomato juice."

Over two-thirds of the women even in the top category who do not drink were very firm in their convictions. "Even if my husband drinks like a fish why should I? I stick to my principles wherever I may be. I do not need drinks to impress others nor to sooth my nerves," was Mrs Gupta's remark. Mrs Prakash felt, "A woman who starts drinking not only loses herself but loses her husband, her home, and her family." "If both the husband and wife began to drink what would happen to the home?" was Mrs Iyer's query.

Areawise there is no great difference in women's attitude to drinking. However, women of the North are more liberal compared to Southern women. More women of the middle socio-economic group of the Central area disapprove of drinking than women of the same strata in other regions.

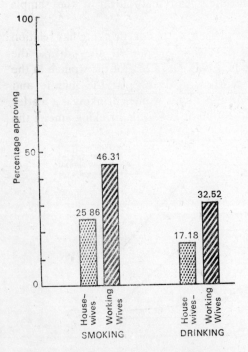

Fig. 25. Approval of smoking and drinking according to occupational status.

Housewives are more conservative in this respect than working

women. Even if their husbands take liquor they often disapprove
of it and use their influence to wean them off drinks. Working
women often themselves drink to ease domestic worries and work
tension. However, some working women, especially those unmarried are very firm about their objections to drinking. As Miss
Mathew said, "I do not approve of drinking, though there is no
one here to check me even if I should do so. My parents are in
Kerala and I am living alone here and have all the freedom I want.
But at the same time I remind myself about an unmarried woman's
basic responsibility and decency. I feel I should be more careful
now, because I am personally responsible to live a decent or
indecent life."

ADDICTION TO DRUGS AND TRANQUILLISERS

Women were asked whether they took any tranquillisers. Though
most women did not even know that they could reduce tension
with tablets, some women, especially in the upper and middle socio-
economic strata, said they took tranquillisers. The use of
tranquillisers is not a regular feature with most Indian women.
98% of the low classes have not known addiction to drugs or
tranquillisers. They chewed pan, took pan with tobacco or rarely
opium but never drugs to relieve tension.

In the middle socio-economic strata over 11% have taken pills
for sleep or for reducing anxiety or worry. In the middle strata
women from the East had the highest number taking tranquillisers,
the least being in the South. Most of those who had tranquillisers
took it as a medicine usually with a doctor's prescription, for
sleeplessness, tension or worry and not as a regular habit.

Women in the higher socio-economic strata of the East and
North are more addicted to tranquillisers than others. Maybe the
fast pace of living especially in the higher strata is responsible for
initiating men and women into drugs for relieving tension and
sleeplessness.

When we consider the use of tension-relieving pills in different
occupational groups we find that when women combine two roles
they are more prone to drugs to reduce tension. Working housewives top the list, though even here the percentage is negligible
compared to the affluent societies. Nearly 90% are never on tranquillisers. Less than 10% take it sometimes. And only a little over

1% take it always. These low figures are encouraging. But when the availability increases and doctors indiscriminately initiate patients on tranquillisers the percentage is sure to increase.

The better educated a woman, the more readily does she resort to artificial methods to lessen her tension. The occasional use of tranquillisers goes up from about 3% in women with primary school education to over 22% among professionals. More than 5% professional women are always on tranquillisers. The greater the academic achievement, or more affluent the status and more challenging a woman's individual life, her worries and problems are proportionately greater. Unless she has the mental stamina and strength to tide over her problems she may find an escape through drugs and tranquillisers. When women were asked why they took tranquillisers various reasons were given—to overcome work tension. to get through crises in love or marriage, to overcome sleeplessness.

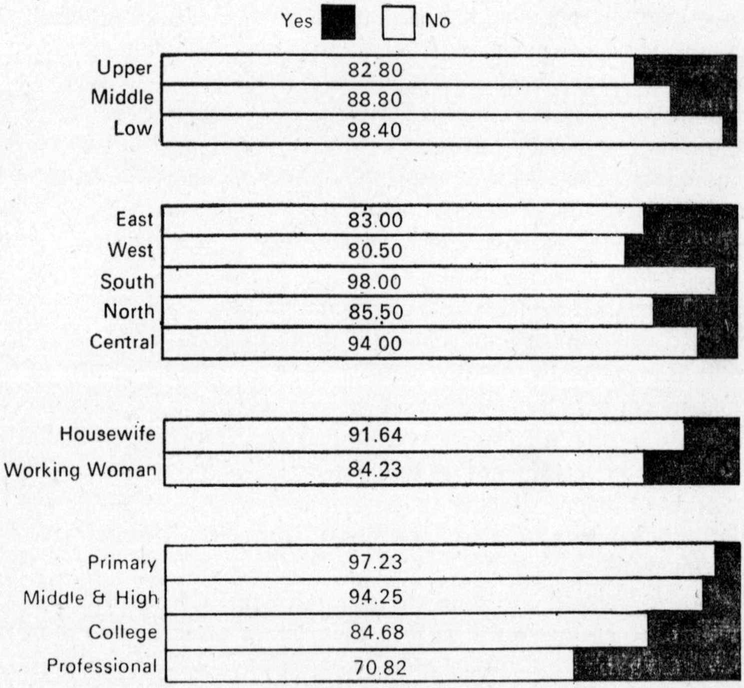

Fig. 26. *Use of tranquillisers according to socio-economic status, **region**, occupational status, and educational level.*

Miss Tata, a working woman, started on tranquillisers to get over an emotional crisis. She has not been able to give up the habit now. Mrs Mitra, an M.A., who always had sleeepless nights started taking pills to get sleep. She has been on them for over four years and is afraid to stop them.

It is interesting to note that more emancipated women become easy victims to artificial modes to relieve tension. The less sophisticated look within to discover their own internal strength to tide over a crisis.

SEVEN

Social Issues

There are many practices in our society which either deal with women in particular or affect all members of the community. Some practices like *purdah* once served a purpose and have now been modified, while others though not particularly beneficial are still kept up due to conservatism. Some are approved by the government, but some are to be abolished by the legislature, for example dowry. Few practices remain as debatable social issues to which people are not sure whether to respond favourably or unfavourably. These include premarital sex, divorce, widow remarriage etc. The present study deals with a few of them.

ATTITUDE TOWARDS DOWRY

The majority of respondents were unfavourable towards dowry which is a burden on the parents. In fact dowry interferes with higher education, which also needs heavy investment. For this reason a girl is generally regarded as a liability. Since the money for dowry has to be saved, a career for girls is not considered necessary or viable. The parents feel the returns from a girl's employment would benefit another family, although it may just as well be the daughter's family who would enjoy the benefit. But the parents will not have any access to the married daughter's earning even if they need it.

The women in this study revolted against the idea of being treated as objects to be married off as early as possible with a dowry. They did not favour the idea of being displayed in the marriage market and evaluated according to the dowry, as personal qualities are then disregarded. One advantage of dowry is that it facilitates the marriage of some girls who could not get married otherwise. The Government of India has not yet formulated definite ideas on how to deal with this social practice.

Nirupama Rao narrated the story of her parents who were living in poverty after getting their four daughters married. Her father, now retired, was working in the P & T Department, and living in Mysore. As dowry was a regular practice in their community, her father was continuously in debt to get his four girls married. "There was a stage when I decided I would never get married. But then I had to think of my younger sister. If I had refused marriage they would have had difficulty in getting her married. As I have seen how much my parents had to suffer to see us married I would never dream of accepting dowry for my two sons."

Vijayalakshmi, who had to delay marriage till she was thirty-two as her parents could not afford a dowry, ended marrying a widower who did not take any dowry. "It is high time the evil of dowry disappeared. No woman can have respect for herself if this practice prevails."

Priya Tej, a young undergraduate, felt there was no great point in women saying they do not approve of dowry. "Young men must come forward and say they will not accept dowry. Once they are definite about the evils of dowry no one can perpetuate this custom which has degraded woman's status."

In all areas dowry is considered unfavourable. Only in the Northern and Central regions, a larger percentage of women are in favour of this practice. In these two areas, the practice of dowry is so ingrained that they consider it a necessity to give daughters their rightful gift when they leave home.

Asha Grover justified her opinion in favour of this custom saying, "The dowry I get at the time of marriage is something I can take with me to my new home with pride. Though as a daughter I am eligible to my father's property, one cannot wage a battle with my brothers in demanding my due share since my parents will have to spend their life time with them. As such, a woman's right for property is only theoretical. In practice a women will get nothing if she loses her right to a dowry."

When we consider the stratification of society socio-economic-ally, the lower strata seemed to be more favourable to the practice of dowry than the other two groups. This underprivileged section is out of touch with current thinking. They only think in terms of

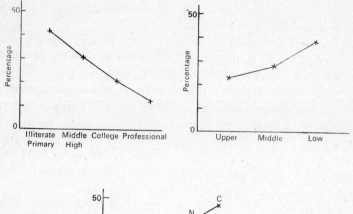

Fig. 27. Percentage of respondents favouring dowry according to education, socio-economic status and region.

the little money they give during the marriage. The practice of dowry as it exists among the higher castes of India is unknown among the lower strata. Very often among the scheduled castes the expenses are equally shared by the bride's and the bridegroom's party. In many hill communities it is the man who gives a "bride price" to be allowed to marry a girl. The acute harassment which high caste middle class families face to get their daughters married is never seen among the lower classes.

It is encouraging to note that the percentage of women favouring dowry is gradually reduced with progressive levels of education. This reveals that the trend in social practices is primarily determined by education in all stratas of society.

ATTITUDE TOWARDS MIXED MARRIAGES

Mixed marriage was considered to be a marriage where caste, religious, or linguistic considerations do not come in. Caste as a barrier to marriage is gradually dying off especially in urban areas since people are more aware of the personality characteristics which are important in making marriage a success. The uprooting of families from their ancestral homes, free intermixing of communities, and trade and occupation not necessarily determined by caste background are all factors which have diluted the importance of caste.

A favourable attitude to mixed marriage has come about with better education. The higher the educational level of women, the higher the score for favourableness. Mainly women below college education are narrow minded and rigid about caste differences. (Table 30). A study of 500 college girls by the Anthropology Department of Calcutta University also revealed that 80% favour such marriages.

Table 30

ATTITUDE TOWARDS MIXED MARRIAGE ACCORDING TO EDUCATIONAL LEVEL

Attitude	Less than primary		Middle and high		College		Professional		Total	
	No.	%	No.	%	No.	%	No	%	No.	%
Unfavourable	194	76.68	168	64.37	147	34.10	10	18.18	519	51.90
Favourable	59	23.32	93	35.63	284	65.90	45	81.82	481	48.10
Total	253	100.00	261	100.00	431	100.00	55	100.00	1,000	100.00

Women with lesser education invariably come from conservative families where caste still determines the mode of life, habits and practices. It is very difficult for them to conceive of a society where caste does not exist. Marriage being the basis of family life is fitted into a particular caste pattern when the husband and wife belong to the same caste. A bride and bridegroom belonging to different castes would create innumerable problems it is believed.

When women begin to take up employment their attitude to

caste gets less rigid. Approximately 20% more working women
are favourable towards mixed marriage than housewives. Non-
working women more often have strictly arranged marriages which
conform to all regulations and norms of society. Working wives
are more exposed to the outer world which promotes love marriages.
The difference in attitude between housewives and working wives
towards mixed marriages is shown in the table below.

Table 31

ATTITUDE TOWARDS MIXED MARRIAGE ACCORDING
TO OCCUPATIONAL SIATUS

Attitude	Occupational status			
	Housewife		Working wife	
	No.	%	No.	%
Unfavourable	399	61.76	83	40.88
Favourable	247	38.24	120	59.12
Total	646	100.00	20 }	100.00

Though there is larger approval for mixed marriages among the
better educated and working women, only a few of the rest show a
positive approach to the abolition of caste barriers in marriage.
Very few said that they would encourage their childern to marry
outside the caste. The usual words were, "If my son or daughter
wants to marry outside the caste I have no objection." The women
who themselves had a mixed marriage were more positive in their
approach to such a marriage.

As the pattern in India is still of arranged marriages, caste considerations become a major factor. It is only very rarely that
arranged marriages turn out to be mixed. The new trend, especially
among the educated, for love marriage completely overshadows
caste considerations. When intellectual and emotional compatibility come in, caste becomes secondary. As caste and language
produce great differences in habits, customs, and in life style,
unless men and women are educated, the squeamish attitude towards caste will not completely disappear.

ATTITUDE TOWARDS DIVORCE

Divorce was not heard of in traditional families. In ancient India the belief was such that men and women once united by God should not be separated. With growing individualism one thinks of what is accep able to oneself, not in terms of what is acceptable to society. This attitude obviously makes room for divorce. A divorce is a legal proce s a couple goes through in order to change their ob igations and privileges towards one another and which restores the freedom to remarry. The chief grounds for divorce are licentiousness, adultery, incompatibility, and desertion, communication of venereal disease, excessive drinking, leprosy, religious conversion and impotency. In western countries, according to Alfred Kinsey and Dr Dumas, adultery is common and it is even accepted by society. Some feel that it helps the marriage to relieve pressure on one's spouse who has to provide the sole source of attention, affection and physical love. The present study shows that only the higher socio-economic class tend to think of divorce as somewhat favourable when required (Fig. 28).

The middle and lower socio-economic class are more traditional in their approach and are not fabourable towards divorce under any circumstances. The primary reason for this might be the financial dependency of the female on the male. If they are separated, the family will suffer. The care of children will be hampered. The girl will be a burden on her family again which is not a happy situation in the presence of sisters-in-law in the family. So women are expected to suppress their griefs and stay back with their husbands for the prestige of their family and also to conform to society's expectations. Many times it is unfortunate that the woman is viewed as the cause of the divorce because she is considered to be the person for making adjustments always. If she deviates a little, then she is considered to be at fault. In the upper class the attitude to divorce is almost half on either side of the continum. Some feel it should not be undertaken while others feel that is not worthwhile to waste a lifetime if married life becomes unhappy.

Approval of divorce is directly linked with the educational level of women. As the educational level increases, more and more women approve of divorce if conditions of married life are not congenial. This is especially true of professionals because of their financial independence. They have the confidence, are less tradition-bound and willing to accept change. On the whole the acceptance is slightly over 30%, and for professionals the percentage of acceptance is double that of the average for the whole sample. The study of Calcutta University girls also shows that 76% are against divorce.

Kavita Kothari, who runs a tutorial school, confidently said, "I

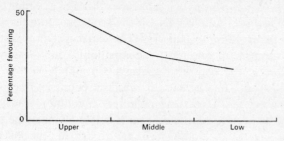

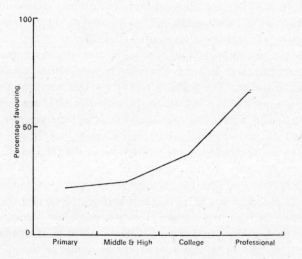

Fig. 28. Attitude to divorce in relation to socio-economic status and education.

do not think I am in any way badly off because I am a divorcee. Just because others think divorce to be wrong and women to be helpless, I cannot spend a lifetime with a man I do not love. Charity begins at home. My own happiness comes before every other consideration. When I am not happily married I cannot maintain the marital partnership."

Men and women become more and more individualistic with education, affluence, and independence. The divorced woman is

naturally more liberal in her attitude to divorce. Among the respondents we had two women divorced twice and two divorcees
unhappy in their second marriage also.

Those who favoured divorce gave numerous reasons for which
a divorce could be considered justified. Some of them are severe
problems with in-laws which make a girl's life miserable; a cruel
and aggressive husband; an alcoholic husband; sexual infidelity;
husband's failure to support his wife and children; when the girl
and her parents are harassed for more money; and when the
husband takes another wife or deserts his wife.

Surprisingly, mental illness or any disease were not mentioned
as legitimate reasons for divorce.

Those against divorce were firm about the need to preserve a
marriage against all odds. The objections against divorce were
that men and women in their foolishness cannot break up homes
and leave children in the lurch; women who are dependent on their
husbands would have no place to go if marriages break up; a
women who leaves one man will never be able to settle down with
another if she has children; divorce is just not acceptable to the
Indian way of life; and as woman always makes the greater adjustment she should preserve the marriage partnership without magni-
fying little problems.

ATTITUDE TOWARDS MARRYING A DIVORCEE

Mrs Vimla Jain said, "I would rather remain unmarried than
marry a man who has left his wife," echoing the views of most
Indian women.

Marrying a divorcee is objectionable to most Indian women but
the attitude is changing with education. Society looks down upon
divorcees, hence a divorced male or female finds it very difficult to
get a suitable match. Often too much emphasis it put on a person's
married life rather than on the individual's merits. Even among
the highly educated only around one-third favour marrying a
divorcee. Among the rest, less than 20% have a favourable attitude.

Miss Raji Viswanath had an interesting explanation for her
preferring a divorcee to a widower. She said, "A divorcee must
have separated from his wife after a quarrel or a misunderstanding.
He cannot have fond feelings for the wife whom he has decided to
separate from. On the other hand a widower must have loving

Table 32

ATTITUDE TOWARDS MARRYING A DIVORCEE IN RELATION TO EDUCATIONAL LEVEL

Attitude	Illiterate & primary		Middle & High		College		Professional		Total	
	No.	%	No.	%	No.	%	No.	%	No.	%
Unfavourable	207	81.81	210	80.45	294	68.21	39	70.91	750	75.00
Farourable	47	18.19	51	19.55	137	31.79	16	29.09	250	25.00

Table 33

ATTITUDE TOWARDS MARRYING A DIVORCEE IN RELATION TO REGION AND SOCIO-ECONOMIC STATUS

Responses	East		West		South		North		Central		Total	
	No.	%	No.	%	No.	%	No.	%	No.	%	No.	%
Upper												
No	40	80.00	39	78.00	36	72.00	39	78.00	42	84.00	196	78.40
Yes	10	20.00	11	22.00	14	28.00	11	22.00	8	16.00	54	21.60
Middle												
No	76	76.00	77	77.00	82	82.00	78	78.00	83	83.00	396	79.20
Yes	24	24.00	23	23.00	18	18.00	22	22.00	17	17.00	104	20.80
Low												
No	31	62.00	35	70.00	30	60.00	31	62.00	31	62.00	158	63.20
Yes	19	38.00	15	30.00	20	40.00	19	38.00	19	38.00	92	36.80
Total												
No	147	73.50	151	75.50	148	74.00	148	74.00	156	78.00	750	75.00
Yes	53	26.50	49	24.50	52	26.00	52	26.00	44	22.00	250	25.00

Table 34

ATTITUDE TOWARDS MARRYING A WIDOWER IN RELATION TO SOCIO-ECONOMIC STATUS AND LEVEL OF EDUCATION

Response	Illiterate & primary		Middle & high		College		Professional		Total	
	No.	%	No.	%	No.	%	No.	%	No.	%
Upper										
No	1	50.00	19	59.38	60	38.55	16	43.24	105	42.00
Yes	1	50.00	13	40.62	110	61.45	21	56.76	145	58.00
Middle										
No	27	54.00	107	58.47	133	53.42	12	66.67	279	55.80
Yes	23	46.00	76	41.53	116	46.58	6	33.33	221	44.20
Low										
No	101	50.25	19	41.30	—	—	—	—	120	48.00
Yes	100	49.75	27	58.70	3	100.00	—	—	130	52.00
Total										
No	129	50.98	145	55.55	102	46.84	28	50.90	504	50.40
Yes	124	49.02	116	44.45	229	53.16	27	49.10	496	49.60
Grand total	253	100.00	261	100.00	431	100.00	55	100.00	1000	100.00

memories of his wife. Such a person will never be able to give any love to his second wife. So I prefer a divorcee to a widower."

There is not much regional variation in the attitude towards marrying a divorcee. But according to the difference in the socio-economic status it is found that the lower socio-economic classes are more favourable towards marrying a divorcee than the middle or higher strata (Tables 32 and 33). Women of the lowest social order often overlook social restrictions for the necessity of survival. As we go up the social ladder, people become more tradition bound, especially the middle classes. Women prefer to maintain the status quo than go against tradition and get ostracised.

ATTITUDE TOWARDS MARRYING A WIDOWER

Only 50% of women accepted marrying a widower. The respondents who favoured this said, "A widower should be willing to compromise. He must not be too old or narrow minded. He must know the practical problems in a second marriage and must be willing to adjust and accomodate." Many women felt a widower could be trusted but not a divocree.

In some cases a widower is accepted for various reasons. The girl may be poor or have some physical defect, and in some cases may be quite old.

Women with college level education in the top strata are more favourable towards marrying a widower than others. In the lower level as well, very often for economic reasons a woman may be willing to compromise. In the upper strata marrying a widower does not seem to be unacceptable.

The middle class is more conservative, and more prove to follow the traditional pattern of marriage. This is the group that is most tradition bound and unwilling to take a chance and accept a new practice. Only out of dire necessity will they compromise.

The respondents revealed a number of reasons for not wanting to marry a widower. He might be an unlucky person, and it would not be wise to link one's fate to his. Also if it could be avoided why should one consider an already married man? Most felt that a widower should marry only a widow as both are in a similar situation. Children from a previous marriage could also create problems. Whatever a woman may do for a widower and his children, a woman becomes a stepmother which is not a very enviable position.

Table 35

ATTITUDE TOWARDS WIDOW REMARRIAGE IN RELATION TO SOCIO-ECONOMIC AND EDUCATIONAL LEVELS

Response	Illiterate & primary		Middle & high school		College		Professional		Total	
	No.	%	No.	%	No.	%	No.	%	No.	%
High										
No	1	50.00	9	28.13	19	10.61	2	5.41	31	12.40
Yes	1	50.00	23	71.87	160	89.39	35	84.59	219	87.60
Middle										
No	22	44.00	68	37.16	50	20.08	1	5.55	141	28.20
Yes	28	56.00	115	62.84	199	79.92	17	94.45	359	71.80
Low										
No	94	46.77	8	17.39	1	33.33	—	—	103	41.20
Yes	107	53.23	38	82.61	2	66.67	—	—	147	58.80
Total										
No	117	42.68	85	32.56	70	16.24	3	5.45	275	27.50
Yes	136	57.32	176	67.44	361	83.76	52	94.55	725	72.50
Grand total	253	100.00	261	100.00	431	100.00	55	100.00	1000	100.00

Some respondent sfelt that a widower remarries out of necessity and not for love. Also, the second wife has a superstitious fear of the spirit of the first wife. Thus, although women in general accepted widow remarriage, they are not very favourable towards marrying a widower.

WIDOW REMARRIAGE

A widower's re-marrying is accepted by society, as he needs help to manage the house. But widow remarriage is looked down upon as a betrayal. The restrictions become more binding in the more conservative groups. However, over 70% of the whole sample

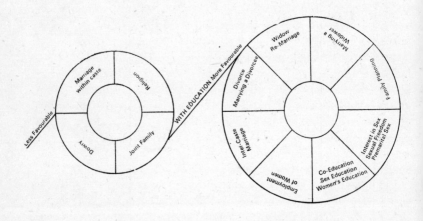

Fig. 29. Attitudinal change with education.

approve widow remarriage. The percentage increases as the educational level and socio-economic status improves (Table 35).

The reasons for opposing widow remarriage were many as stated by the respondents. They felt they were handicapped rather than benefitted by a second marriage. Many felt that the second husband can never take the place of the first. He will never accept her children as his own. So why create more problems? Some women strongly protested against widow remarriage arguing that a woman should marry only once to safeguard the interest of the home and family. Mrs Prasad said with much pride, "A Hindu woman

marries only once. It is a man who needs to marry repeatedly."
Some felt that a widow should not marry if she had the means to
live or the earning capacity. Kamala, a working woman in the lower
income group, said, "What guarantee is there that the second
husband will not die prematurely? If one's husband dies, a woman
should learn to take up a job and make a living. One cannot forget
within a short while the man with whom one has lived and go
around looking for another man after his death. The new husband
may take me but will he take my four children also?"

In contrast to this some women approved widow remarriage.
They gave strong arguments in its favour, saying when a man can
remarry, why not a woman? If a man can remarry and forget the
past why should a woman sacrifice the rest of her life for a
mere memory. Hence the feeling is that it is better that a woman
should remarry and settle down rather than be at a lose end. She
and her children will be better cared for if she remarries and has
a proper home. The favourable attitude towards widow remarriage
is seen more among the educated and the working women.

Those who accepted widow remarriage conditionally said that
widow remarriage is good only if the widow is young or has no
children. Indian women in general are more concerned about the
children rather than their own interest. The fear that a widow's
children will not find a sympathetic father is deep rooted. Many
women were of the conviction that marriage is for a lifetime and if
it ends prematurely, it should be accepted as one's "karma".

For Indian women, especially the less educated, to whatever
strata they may belong to, marriage is a divinely ordained partnership for the good of the family, home, and children rather than for
personal pleasure and happiness. The idea that a woman should
make a greater sacrifice than a man is deeply ingrained They feel
economic emancipation gained by employment outside the home
is more important than looking for opportunities for remarriage.
That is why we see many widows and divorcees taking up gainful
employment especially after the death or seperation of the husband.
Among educated women, fear of loneliness and the need for companionship motivate them for remarriage.

ADOPTION OF CHILDREN

In Indian families childlessness is considered a curse. If there are no children usually the woman is considered responsible. Whatever the case may be, adoption of children is considered an issue to be sorted out in each of these families. Over 50% of women are in favour of adoption (Table 36), but they usually prefer to adopt relatives than orphans. The advantage of adopting relatives is that

Table 36

ATTITUDE TOWARDS ADOPTION OF CHILDREN

Responses	No.	%
Unfavourable	451	45.10
Favourable	549	54.90
Total	1000	100.00

they know the background and would definitely have greater affection because of blood relationship. Some favour adopting orphans because there would be no other claim later and also one can bring up the child the way one likes without interference. The attitude towards adoption did not vary according to socio-economic status or education or the type of family background. However, it was found that the middle class was more conservative than the other two strata.

SEXUAL FREEDOM

The women in this study were asked to air their views about sexual freedom for men and women. It is found that in all classes, the attitude towards sexual freedom is unfavourable. Only slightly over 10% were favourable towards this in the overall sample. In the high socio-economic class 18% approved of it. Even among upper class educated women, the percentage approving of sexual freedom is only about 20%. When the educational level is low, even in the high socio-economic strata the percentage drops to 6%. The women of the middle socio-economic level are uniformly conservative in all levels of education (Table 37).

In spite of education and wealth, Indian women are basically orthodox compared to their western counterparts. Women would rather be conservative than exercise freedom which may result in an unstable life. The more freedom one enjoys, the higher is the

Table 37

ATTITUDE TOWARDS SEXUAL FREEDOM

Response	Level of education									
	Illiterate & primary		Middle & high school		College		Professional		Total	
	No.	%	No.	%	No.	%	No.	%	No.	%
Upper										
Unfavourable	2	100.00	30	93.75	143	79.89	30	81.08	205	82.00
Favourable	—	—	2	6.25	36	20.11	7	18.92	45	18.00
Total	2	100.00	32	100.00	179	100.00	37	100.00	250	100.00
Middle										
Unfavourable	49	98.00	168	91.80	224	89.96	17	94.44	458	91.60
Favourable	1	2.00	15	8.20	25	10.04	1	5.56	42	8.40
Total	50	100.00	183	100.00	249	100.00	18	100.00	500	100.00
Low										
Unfavourable	183	91.04	40	86.96	3	100.00	—	—	226	90.40
Favourable	18	8.96	6	13.04	—	—	—	—	24	9.60
Total	201	100.00	46	100.00	3	100.00	—	—	250	100.00
Unfavourable	234	92.49	238	91.18	370	85.25	47	85.45	889	88.90
Favourable	19	7.51	23	8.82	61	14.75	8	14.55	111	11.10
Grand total	253	100.00	261	100.00	431	100.00	55	100.00	1000	100.00

divorce rate.

The average figure for the sample as a whole is 11%. This is low compared to the statistics available in western countries. Among the three strata surveyed, the lower socio-economic group approve of this more than the other two groups in spite of the fact that the same group put greater restrictions on girls during their early years. After marriage due to environmental reasons some of them are forced to change their attitudes to life and life situations.

The woman of the lower strata make concessions in their standards about sex practices often out of economic necessity. Hafisabi, a prostitute, defended woman's right to sexual freedom. "I have been doing this job for the last 20 years of my life. I have come to believe that any means is justifiable if it is to fill one's belly. When my husband drove me out and took another wife no one came forward to help me. I ran away from the village to earn my living and support myself and my daughter in this big city. I could not find employment in a house as a servant or as a cook as I had a child with me. An old lady whose acquaintance I made started me on this profession."

Any woman who has broken away from the tetherings of normal domestic life becomes liberal in her attitude to sexual freedom. She realises there cannot be different standards for man and for woman. Sexual freedom is more often approved by emancipated women belonging to the progressive younger group, by woman unhappy in marriage, sexually frustrated, widowed, or separated. A woman who finds complete fulfilment in her marital life rarely advocates sexual licence for women.

Mrs Meneziz strongly felt that women must enjoy the same liberties which a man enjoys. "I would say it is my husband who had made me immoral. I lived seven years with him without seeing day of happiness. He drank, gambled, went to women, squandered even what I earned. I moved over to mother's house with my two boys four years ago. Now I have no compunction to go with any man if he gives me money. With my salary alone I cannot support my two boys and pay for the maintenance of my mother who is dependent on me. I would rather live this life of sin than go back to my husband."

Rama Devi, a prostitute, blamed her husband for showing her the easy way to sell herself for money. "My husband compelled me to sleep with the men he brought home because they were willing to pay him. Now he stays home with my one year old daughter when I roam the streets at night." When asked, "Doesn't your husband mind your going to different men?" Rama Devi snapped, "Why should he? He gets money for drinks and he is happy. If I find a man who will support me and my child, I will give up this occupation and run away."

Women who have gone through marital insecurity or economic distress often find sexual liberty a convenient tool to make a living. The degradation they have gone through makes them take a very loose attitude to sex.

On the other hand a woman's personal failure to have a successful married life might make her take a very rigid attitude to sexual freedom for women. Herabai, the mistress of a rich businessman, had a tragedy to reveal. She comes from a family which has practised prostitution for generations. She never wanted to be a prostitute but she had no choice as she was introduced into the profession by her mother when she was hardly 16. After living a life of vice for over 15 years she met Mr M who took her as his permanent 'keep' and brought her over to Calcutta. He maintains her and provides for her needs. She has two children, a girl and a boy. She would never want her daughter to undergo what she has gone through in life. She hopes her daughter will get married into a good home and live the life of a normal woman.

Some women with lax morals become so out of necessity. They are the victims of social discrimination, oppression and ostracism. They are the products of a rigid conservative order which discriminates against women because of their sex. Such women, be they widows, victims of forcible child marriage, deserted women, or illegitimate mothers, find the cover of sexual licence very convenient to sustain themselves in a society where they are not wanted.

Now let us see why in our society women in general do not approve of sexual freedom for men and women. Mrs Rao declared, "Woman makes a home. If she becomes immoral the home will go to ruins. A woman with character not only retains her dignity but invariably influences her husband to be straight. Both men and women have to exercise sexual restraint if they have to preserve the home."

Latha Chellam, a graduate in literature said, "Woman cannot use the same yardstick as a man to decide her sex values. Often sex means so little to a respectble woman, and it is love which matters—an emotional experience involving her so completely that she gets totally immersed in her family life. Just because man is basically polygamous, woman cannot waiver sexual restraint and follow him. Standards of permissiveness for men and women are bound to be different."

Mrs Sethi disapproves of sexual freedom for women. "I believe in women getting education, taking up jobs, earning for the family but not going wild sexually simply because men also enjoy sexual freedom. Our society has remained stable because of women's regard for their home, family and reputation."

The concept of *pativrata*—a woman's complete loyalty to the man she marries—is deep rooted in the minds of Indian women, and they are convinced that sex should be limited to the marriage partnership. They are not eager to compete with men in this respect. "So what if men enjoy sexual freedom" is the attitude of many. The average woman is more concerned with playing the role of an ideal mother, a wife who will remain pure even if the husband errs. She is against taking sexual liberties for her personal gratification.

When the social status is high and the woman is well educated and young she takes a liberal view towards sex. Even if social norms are broken she feels less alienated. Money and position compensate for other values.

Boy Friends

A majority of women had not known any male closely enough to be classed as a boy friend. Although around 17% mentioned a boy friend, the degree of intimacy they had with the male friend varied considerably. For some it was just an adolescent crush, looking into each other's eyes or steathily holding hands. In others it was their first and last love as they had loved the man and married him. Those who have enjoyed sexual freedom before do not necessarily marry the man with whom they had an affair and remain romantically inclined to men even after marriage. There were a few who had boy friends regularly for the sake of fun. More women in the educated group had boy friends, probably because women of this group get an opportunity to mix with men in college or at their place of work. Approximately one-third of the professional women had boy friends in the upper and middle socio-economic strata (Table 38).

In the lower socio-economic strata, even when the educational

Table 38

HAVING BOY FRIENDS IN DIFFERENT SOCIO-ECONOMIC CLASS BY EDUCATION

Response	Illiterate & primary		Middle & high school		College		Professional		Total	
	No.	%	No.	%	No.	%	No.	%	No.	%
Upper										
No	2	100.00	28	87.50	127	70.95	24	64.86	181	72.40
Yes	—	—	4	12.50	52	29.05	13	35.14	69	27.60
Middle										
No	50	100.00	164	89.62	204	81.93	13	72.22	431	86.20
Yes	—	—	19	10.38	45	18.07	5	27.78	69	13.80
Low										
No	174	86.56	36	78.26	3	100.00	—	—	213	85.20
Yes	27	13.44	10	21.74	—	—	—	—	37	14.80
Total										
No	226	89.32	220	87.35	334	77.49	37	67.28	825	82.50
Yes	27	10.68	33	12.65	97	22.51	18	32.72	175	17.50

level is only up to high school, slightly over 20% had boy
friends. However, the proportion is very small in comparison to
the western countries. Yet, for a conservative and tradition oriented society like ours, even this proportion is surprising. In the
urban complex, many social restrictions and taboos have lesser
effect because of environmental factors. Young people study together where they get plenty of opportunity to mix. When residential
areas are crowded, one gets an opportunity to come into contact
with men. Among women of the upper strata, where western standards are often adopted, having a boy friend, sometimes even
after marriage, becomes part of life. In the lowest lot, young
women coming from unhappy homes or separated girls easily fall
prey to sex.

Anasuya, who is separated from her husband, works as a full-
time domestic servant. She became sexually intimate with Hari
Singh, a Bihari driver, and married him.

Widow Sundari Bai had in her youth many boy friends. Her
husband was nearly 20 years older to her. When she got married
she was 15 and her husband over 35. She had four children. When
he died after a short illness she started living with a friend of her
husband in order to support herself and her children, and had two
more children. When this man deserted her she lost all moral value
and sold herself frequently for money. Though free dating is un-
popular in India, women have boy friends. Some have even openly
lived with the man they have loved. In exceptional cases, especially
if marital happiness is denied, a woman has repeatedly sold herself for monetary purposes.

Premarital Sex

Indian women are still conservative about premarital sex. Only
the better educated women belonging to the upper socio-economic
strata make some concession in this matter. They are the educated
group who are economically independent. They have probably
been free with men, loved and married the man of their choice. If
not married they probably would like to move with men and make
their own selection.

Some women feel there is no harm in being sexually intimate
with the man one loves and proposes to marry. Educated women
are well acquainted with family planning methods and are capable
of protecting themselves against undesired pregnancy. 93% of

Table 39

APPROVAL OF PREMARITAL SEX IN THE DIFFERENT SOCIO-ECONOMIC CLASSES IN RELATION TO EDUCATIONAL LEVEL

Response	Illiterate & primary		Middle or high school		College		Professional		Total	
	No.	%	No.	%	No.	%	No.	%	No.	%
Upper										
No	2	100.00	30	93.75	155	86.59	28	75.48	215	86.00
Yes	—	—	2	6.25	24	13.41	9	24.32	35	14.00
Middle										
No	50	100.00	176	96.17	230	92.37	17	94.45	473	94.60
Yes	—	—	7	3.83	19	7.63	1	5.56	27	5.40
Low										
No	192	95.52	43	93.47	3	100.00	—	—	238	95.20
Yes	9	4.48	3	6.53	—	—	—	—	12	4.80
Total										
No	244	96.44	249	95.02	388	92.02	45	81.81	926	92.60
Yes	9	3.56	12	4.98	43	9.98	10	18.19	74	7.40
Grand Total	253	100.00	261	100.00	431	100.00	55	100.00	1000	100.00

respondents do not approve of premarital sex.

The professionals in this group scored the highest percentage with 25% favouring sex before marriage. These women felt it was better to establish sexual compatibility before marriage rather than regretting it later. Education gives woman the freedom to decide what she needs, and this is especially true for the professionally qualified. The middle and lower classes fit into a more conservative pattern compared to the upper class.

Except for the highly educated women of the upper strata, sexual freedom before marriage is not socially permitted. Even the question of a girl openly dating a boy does not arise, and it is usually done stealthily without the knowledge of the family members. Rekha Naik put this question, "When we are not even allowed to talk freely with boys where does the question of sex experience come in? I am now 19. I go to a college for women. Except for a few of my brother's friends with whom I talk, I have not known any boy intimately. If I have to see a movie or go to a restaurant I usually go with my girl friends."

In the lower levels of urban society, because of the severe uprooting which most of the families go through people tend to become less conservative. Morals become lax especially if the girl is a little educated or is employed and economically independent.

Kavita Mondal, an unmarried girl working at a milk booth has had sex experience. She was ashamed to admit that often she got money from men she slept with. She had very little choice in the matter. The meagre amount of Rs 110 she earned from her job was insufficient to support her mother, two brothers, and two sisters. Her widowed mother was not rich enough to marry her off. Mrs Meera Das, a divorcee, said she had sex experience before marriage with a man whom she wanted to marry very much. Unfortunately her family never approved of the match. She was forced to marry a man of her parents' choice. The marriage was never happy, and after four years she separated.

In general, the Indian woman grows in a conservative background where woman does not enjoy sexual freedom. Even sexual licence in men is not really accepted because of the importance attached to sexual restraint before marriage both in men and women. Does the Indian woman mentally accept the idea of sex before marriage? Is she trying to bring a change in favour of sexual freedom for woman?

The Indian marriage continues to be a sacrament, a partnership for a lifetime. Chastity and virginity are still held with the greatest respect. Marriage in most cases initiates a woman into sex. She has neither the right nor desire to flout sex before marriage, and the more conservative the group the more fixed this idea becomes.

EIGHT

Employment

The status of Indian women has undergone a gradual evolution. The privileged position of women in the Vedic period was completely changed in the dark ages that followed. The woman was kept in bonds, solely a begetter of children and a housekeeper. Man in return provided her with protection and economic support. Thus her economic and social freedom became progressively jeopardised.

Discrimination on the basis of sex became the order of the day. Repression started with the general notion that certain characteristics were considered a monopoly of the male. She was even conditioned to look down on herself and submit herself to the acknowledged superiority of the male. She was led to underestimate her own potential and submit herself totally to the demands of her family.

The principle of equality has remained primarily a theoretical one. Our society has hitherto failed to realise that the participation of women in economic, social and political life will further the cause of progress in developing nations. If men try to ascend the economic ladder at the expense of women, progress will be partial at most. Raising the level of skill and the aspirations of both men and women is necessary for a developing nation. The conviction will bring about the emancipation of women in the true sense. The movement for women's emancipation in India is not directed against men. The movement is aimed at utilising the untapped resource of half the population of the country, which if not utilised will make the country poorer.

The fundamental difficulty faced by working women is the fact that there are bound to be certain differences inherent in the sex. Married women unlike men will probably have to interrupt their careers to bring up the family, depending on the circumstances, and on that basis they would be discriminated against in spite of the fact that in theory she is allowed the most advanced legal and constitutional right of equality. Women are also assumed to be emotional in the sense of not having the capacity to control or channelise their emotions in productive ways.

Since the feminine and professional role expectations are pictured by society as being mutually exclusive, one might think that women who are career-minded are not feminine. Thus there is so much ambivalence and disapproval facing women who wish to be gainfully employed. Thus, in spite of the fact that women have a favourable attitude towards gainful employment, the attitude of society is obstructive.

In 1964, the Labour Bureau undertook the collection and analysis of all the available material on this issue and published a report entitled "Women in Employment." The report gave a brief account of the trends in women's employment as revealed by the information gathered through various sources such as census data, the second Agricultural Labour Enquiry, the return received under the Factories and the Mines Acts, information collected in respect of plantations, information gathered and supplied by the Directorate General of Employment and Training under the employment market information scheme, and data collected by the Bureau on the extent of women's employment. The report revealed that by and large there had been a perceptible increase both in the number of female employees and in the industrial and occupational categories in which they were being steadily absorbed. While the position in the traditional industries had not recorded any appreciable change either way; many fresh avenues of employment have opened up for women in recent years, and according to the estimates made by the Planning Commission there is still considerable room for the absorption of women in gainful employment.

Kamala Nath pointed out that female workers constitute only one-third of the total work-force of the country. Of all female workers 93 3% are in rural areas and only 6% are in urban areas. The 1972 census shows that out of the 264 million female population, 132 millions are between 14 and 50 and out of that only 2,796,60) constitute the female working force. Half of them are agricultural labourers, one third of them cultivators, a few in subsidiary fishing, hunting etc., and the rest are distributed among all the other occupational categories.

Nearly 82% of women in India are engaged in agricultural and other allied occupations which they have been doing from time immemorial. They have been partners of their menfolk. The proportion of female earnings to male earnings in agricultural employment shows that Bihar tops the list with 84.4%, followed by Madhya Pradesh 83.5%. Mysore 78.10%, Assam 77.5% and Orissa 73.20%. Karnataka is the only state of India which has a high literacy rate and high female work participation (See S.M Pandey, *Wage, Income,Expenditure,and Indebtedness of Agricultural Labourers in India*, National Commission on Agriculture, New Delhi, 1974).

In all areas of the unorganised sector there is clear discrimination against female labour. The rate of employment before independence was about 39% and in 1971 it had come down to 17%. The decline in participation in the labour force by women is actually threatening the upliftment of women's status. If equality of opportunity is cherished as a major step for progress, this group should not be denied opportunities which are available. It would be a great loss to the world to leave these potentially capable women unemployed.

The great majority of women workers in India are engaged in either agriculture or traditional rural industries and in service occupations. The work participation rate of urban women is significantly lower than that of rural women, and that of literate women lower than that of illiterate women. One possible reason for this might be that still many men are critical of the idea of their wives working and say that in the case of a working wife and mother the care and development of children is hampered and husband-wife ties are weakened. Wives being employed is not only disapproved in principle by many husbands but it is highly threatening for some. For some men employed wives imply their own failure in their role fulfilment to themselves, to the family and the community at large.

The present study reveals some of the salient points regarding working women and their attitude towards their work. In the present study working-wives constitute about 20% of the sample, the figure tallying with the national figure for employment of women. According to the socio-economic classification it is found that only

18.80% of them work in the upper category, 13.60% in the middle category, and 35% in the lowest one. This shows that the illiterate

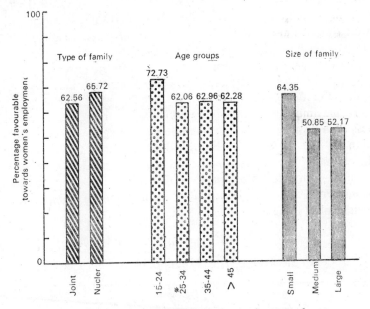

Fig. 30. Percentage of respondents favouring employment of women according to type of family, age, and size of family.

lower class forms the major part of the labour force than women from the other classes. A study of the types of jobs held by women shows that 36.95% women were employed as servants, 26.30% as teachers, 13.70% as secretaries, 9.30% as cooks and tailors, 7.80% as nurses and welfare officers, 4.70% as doctors, lawyers and engineers, and 1.20% as beauticians and hair dressers.

The lower strata women seek employment purely for economic reasons. An interview with Naniwal Das, a domestic servant, revealed that she would not take up employment outside home if her husband could earn a sufficient wage. "Because we have no money for the expenses of the family, I have to substitute his pay by looking after other people's children." In fact a subtle feeling of jealousy is indicated in some of the responses. Middle class women are economically better off than the lower income category and hence are not required to work if they do not want to. But they are expected to do all the housework and thus save money to provide for other necessities. The upper class women are more free in their choice to take up work than the middle class women and perhaps better qualified also. Considering the statistics for working women we find that in the upper and middle category in which women are better educated, the rate of employment is also proportionately higher. Education makes them more employable hence they get more job opportunities. But in the lower strata job opportunities are fixed and educational qualifications becomes quite redundant.

A maximum percentage of working wives are in the group with less than primary education, the rate decreasing in direct proportion to the increase in educational level. Among the housewives, less than 3% are professionally qualified. Since the number of women with adequate education and skill are still comparatively few, there is lesser participation by women in the comparatively better jobs (Table 40).

Table 40

OCCUPATIONAL STATUS ACCORDING TO EDUCATION

Educational level	Housewives		Working wife	
	No.	%	No.	%
More than primary	152	23.52	77	37.92
Middle & high	207	32.05	30	14.77
College	270	41.79	68	33.49
Professionals	17	2.64	28	13.82

In the upper strata, women without education do not look for work, but those with college education and professional qualification would like to engage themselves in partial or full employment, the respective statistics being 90% of the professionals 60% of the college educated women. The same is true for middle class families also. In the lower classes, with the lowest level of education, aspiration for work is lacking. Many of the lower class married women would not work had it not been for economic needs.

Women who were not employed were asked about their attitude towards outside work. In accordance with the type of family they came from, it was found that half the women from nuclear families would like to work, compared to only one-third of women from joint families. This shows that women from nuclear families, though they have no one to share family responsibilities, would still like to work outside home provided there are opportunities. The financial reward they get be invested in their family of procreation itself.

Ranjini Chandra, a graduate, said, "I am looking for a part-time teaching job. Both my children have now started going to school and I am free in the mornings. If I work, it will supplement my husband's income. If nothing comes up I will start giving tuitions." In a joint family, the freedom to act independently is usually lost. Household responsibilities could be more burdensome and the attitude of the family members towards working women might be adverse. Thus they might gradually lose their incentive for any creative work outside their homes. Manorama, a dentist, had to stop working after marriage when she moved into her husband's joint family. Even after five years of marriage she could not get the courage to start on her profession again. Her excuse was, "I am too preoccupied with domestic responsibilities. Besides, my in-laws feel there is no need for me to work as my husband is earning well."

Table 41

WOMEN'S OCCUPATIONAL STATUS AND TYPE OF FAMILY

	Type of family			
Occupational status	*Joint*		*Nuclear*	
	No.	%	*No.*	%
Housewives	252	77.06	393	75.72
Working wives	75	22.94	126	24.28
Total	327	100.00	519	100.00

As seen from the table a slightly higher percentage of women from nuclear families are employed than those in joint families, although the difference is marginal.

Now looking at the type of work preferred by women in different socio-economic classes it was seen that teaching was most preferred. Over 30% of the upper income classes preferred teaching compared to about 25% of the middle class, and 4% in the lowest class. Women from the South and East liked teaching to any other vocations. Taking up a profession was also preferred by the upper income group and then the middle category, but clerical jobs were most desired by the middle class. Domestic work are preferred mostly by the lowest group.

ATTITUDE TOWARDS THE EMPLOYMENT OF MARRIED WOMEN
ON THE BASIS OF REGION AND SOCIO-ECONOMIC STATUS

Views are greatly at variance regarding the employment of married women outside the home. Some think it is acceptable for un-married women to work, but once married the same workers were expected to terminate gainful employment. As a result some dis-continue their employment while others continue their jobs or change the type of job. The personal motivation of the worker must be considered in the broader perspective of social change.

The present study indicates that attitude towards employment is mostly favourable. Over 60% of women are favourably inclined towards this issue when we analyse it on a cross cultural basis. According to the different socio-economic levels, 75% of the upper socio-economic class are favourable as also 60% of the lower income group. But the percentage for the middle income group is still low. In general, the middle class is more conservative and often they are unable to go out to work because of family respon-sibilities and lack of funds to keep proper servants. The percentage for the North and Central regions is also low perhaps due to greater social resistance against the employment of married women. Throughout India, most ayahs working outside their homes are either from the South or from East. One rarely comes across an ayah from Punjab, U.P. or M.P. Even in a family belonging to the lower socio-economic strata a Punjabi woman would rather stay at home and do embroidery or knitting than go out for work. Women

Table 42

PREFERENCE FOR WORK ACCORDING TO THE TYPE OF FAMILY

Response	Type of family			
	Joint		*Nuclear*	
	No.	%	*No.*	%
Not interested to work	173	62.83	241	49.39
Part-time	84	30.21	189	38.73
Full-time	21	6.96	58	11.88
Total	278	100.00	488	100.00

from Madhya Pradesh take up employment out of necessity. In our tradition-bound society it was not considered respectable for a middle or upper class woman, particularly when married, to seek a career or to accept service outside home. It was only under economic pressures that women came out to take up gainful employment.

In the higher socio-economic strata all the areas are progressive to the same extent in their attitude to working women.

Table 43

ATTITUDE TOWARDS EMPLOYMENT OF MARRIED WOMEN
ACCORDING TO REGION AND SOCIO-ECONOMIC STATUS

Region	Socio-economic class							
	Upper		Middle		Low		Total	
	Un-favour-able	Favour-able	Un-favour-able	Favour-able	Un-favour-able	Favour-able	Un-favour-able	Favour-able
	%	%	%	%	%	%	%	%
East	24	76	37	63	30	70	30.33	69.67
West	28	72	37	63	34	66	33.00	67.00
South	26	74	36	64	28	72	30.00	70.00
North	22	78	47	53	36	64	35.00	65.00
Central	26	74	43	57	48	52	39.00	61.00
Mean %	25.20	74.80	40.00	60.00	35.20	64.80	33.46	66.54

The attitude towards employment of women has undergone a remarkable change, and over 66% women are favourable to married women working (Table 43). Even if a woman herself is not employed, she sees no objection to working women as a whole.

Mrs Sudha Murthy, a widow and a mother of four children remarked, "Unfortunately I cannot do anything but domestic work, but I admire a working women who can stand on her own. My daughters are both working, and I hope that even after marriage they will continue."

Mrs Subhra Banerjee, a housewife, also held the same opinion. "Both my daughters-in-law teach, to which we have no objections. I am there to look after the children, so why should they stay home all day and waste their time?"

The employed group more readily accepts the employment of married women than the non-employed group. While over 90% of working women feel there are definite advantages in a wife working, only about 50% of housewives have a similar attitude.

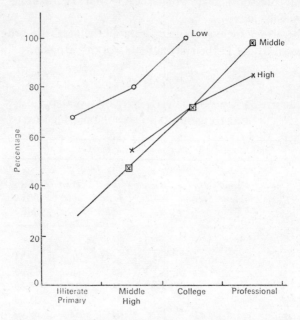

Fig. 31. Attitude towards married women's employment according to education and socio-economic status.

Mrs Kamala completed her S.S.C. but had to discontinue her education in order to get married. She had to wait for eight years before her marriage could be settled. During this period she lost her parents and had to depend on her married brother for a living. She regretfully said, "If only I had taken up employment immediately after school, I would have helped my own family instead of being a burden on them for eight years. Secondly, after marriage whatever income I could fetch home would have been a great help to my husband to run the family. He is only a clerk in a bank. He has two brothers and two sisters to support besides his mother. Now I cannot get a job, since I have no qualifications."

Hearing the stories of some women from the lower classes, one would be convinced that it is essential for these women also to take

Table 44

OCCUPATIONAL STATUS DETERMINING THE ATTITUDE
TOWARDS EMPLOYMENT OF MARRIED WOMEN

Attitude	Housewife		Working wife	
	No.	%	No.	%
Unfavourable	310	47.90	20	9.85
Favourable	336	52.10	183	90.15
Total	646	100.00	203	100.00

up some job for financial security. Neelamma was given in marriage to a widower with one child. Unfortunately, after bearing six children she fell ill for some time and her husband took another wife. Neelamma said, "If I had not taken to work, I would have been on the streets with my children. I worked as a part-time maid servant in three houses and brought up my children. Now my eldest son is a mechanic in a garage and I am dependent on him By working I could support the family till the children are on their own." The plea of another working woman that "every person, man or woman must earn," could be a national policy for the economic development of the individual, community, and the nation.

Working women, married or unmarried, are naturally in favour of women working. However, a woman's opinion often reflects the opinion of her husband or mother-in-law, for instance.

Shila Raj gave up her job in a travel agency to oblige her husband as he felt it would not be possible for a woman to effectively combine domestic obligations with outside employment. Parvathi, a nurse who gave up working after marriage, feels that once a girl is married it becomes difficult for her to take up employment and manage a home. It is better if she plays one role successfully. According to her if a woman is keen on a career, she should not marry.

"I delayed marriage till 34 years of age because I wanted to work for some years to support my parents. This I did for over 15 years. Now that I am married I feel I must devote myself completely to my home, husband, and children."

The student group is less favourable towords women's employment than working women. Some are apprehensive about their capacity to get a job. A few even feel a woman need not necessarily take up a job just because she is educated. Often in India, girls go for college education without the idea of pursuing a career. In certain parts of India graduation is a necessary qualification for marriage.

Sobha Desai, an educated wife from the high income group says, "There is no need for me to work. My husband is doing good business and there is no difficulty as far as money is concerned. I have two young girls. Where do I have the time to go out and work? My family would not mind my doing few hours of social work. But they object to my taking up paid employment. Personally I feel women should take up employment only when there is a necessity. She can always do more at home and help society through social service."

Some women favour employment to utilise their education. Others feel they will earn much more if they are employed, leaving the housework to be done by services. An extremely mistaken notion is that often a woman is made to feel useless if she is only a housewife, because a housewife contributes much more towards the development of a family than a man. Calculating family services in terms of money value done by a wife/mother in U.S.A. revealed, interestingly enough, that it is equal to or more than the money earned by the husband.

The attitude towards the employment of married women in the three different socio-economic groups in relation to the level of education revealed that as the level of education increases, the attitude towards employment also becomes more favourable (Fig. 31). In the case of a lower education in the lower income families, the attitude to women working outside the home was still favourable. Even in this group a favourable attitude increased considerably with education.

The professionally qualified middle income group are very keen on employment as they are highly qualified for a particular career and would like to use their experience for making an income. The middle school and college educated low income group are very much inclined to employment outside the home maybe because of financial necessity and their own progressive outlook in the conservative set-up of the low strata.

The employment of wives would become easier with the absence of pre-school to school-aged children. Many women although unfavourable towards this issue felt that they can work if the children are old enough and do not need the attention of the mother. Other conditional acceptances of maternal employment were in cases of husband not having a job, his illness, extreme financial difficulties, the availability of a suitable part-time job etc.

Considering some of the other factors, like type of family, size of family, and the age group of women, it was found that women in single unit families are definitely a little more progressive than those in joint families (Fig.30).

In spite of a favourable attitude in favour of employment, in some cases it may not be possible for a woman to work because of lack of substitute help at home. This problem is particularly significant in small family units. Women from joint families are more fortunate in this respect, as they have the mother-in-law, sister-in-law, aunt or grandmother to take care of the children during their absence from home.

Indu Saigal and Charu Mital were both B. Eds. Indu, who belonged to a nuclear family, was not working as she had three little children below the age of six. She had no dependable help at home and so could not take up a job. Charu, though in a joint family, was teaching as her sister-in-law took care of her two boys while she was away from home. In spite of these problems a woman's personal attitude to work is a greater determinant than the attitude of the family in which she lives. One woman takes up outside employment against all odds while another, in spite of the time and opportunities, stays home engrossed in purely domestic duties.

Neelam Anand, though a professionally qualified doctor, decided against taking up employment because her husband was in a good job in shipping. "There is no need for me to work," she asserted. It is surprising that she did not even think of doing an honorary job which would have given her professional satisfaction even if not money.

The younger generation is more favourable towards employment. They belong to this era of woman's liberation and they feel that they have every right to work as men do. Some of them do not think that it would be difficult to combine both the roles. Generally speaking, smaller families are also more favourable perhaps because of lesser commitments and obligations to the family.

Why People Object to Women Taking up Employment

About 30% of our sample react unfavourably to this issue. Why? Traditionally, they feel the "Lakshmi" of the house should remain at home for the family's welfare. In a rural society men and women work in the fields and contribute to the agricultural economy. With urbanisation man was responsible for work outside the home and women in the house. This became an accepted social norm. Often, even if the women is not employed, she might be spending a lot of time outside home for her own personal enjoyment. The criticism against that is still to be raised. Often there is a stigma attached to woman's employment because if a wife starts working, it might imply that the husband is not fully able to support the family, since it is an accepted fact that the primary reason for woman's employment is economic. Or it might be thought that the mother is neglecting the family. These factors are considered to undermine the status of the family. With the housewife's employment, often childern are neglected and so is the housekeeping. A working woman tends to develop a tendency to dominate over her husband and other members. Sometimes the husband is burdened with household responsiblities due to the wife's employment. When the husband comes back from work, their could be tension if both husband and wife are tired after the day's work. Sometimes the children's education might also suffer as a result.

Since housekeeping is inevitable for married women, many complain that they cannot get the right kind of job which synchronises with domestic duties. Jobs dealing with household duties, private tuitions, consultation work etc. usually suit women. Many office jobs have inconvenient timings which make it impossible for women to combine such jobs with housework. In some cases the transfer of the husband seriously affects a woman's career. Some women might also lack the incentive to work. Since the woman's personal attitude to work is more consequential than other factors or obstacles, it might be more correct to classify women as the working or the non-working type.

There is a general tendency among working women to look down on non-working women as parasites on society. This attitude is most unhealthy. Women who devote their time to the home and give a proper direction to their children are rendering the most valuable service to the family, community and to the nation as a whole, as Mother Teresa pointed out. But this is not recognised by society and hence the status of a housewife is far below that of a working wife. Every woman, educated or not, should have the freedom to choose between a purely domestic role and one where she combines both work and family, or even choose a career at the expense of family life. The antagonism towards a typical domestic role perpetrates a very unhealthy trend in society. In spite of having very heavy domestic responsibilities, a mere housewife often feels she is not spending her life in a worthwile manner. She might envy her friends or relatives who are earning like men. In contrast to this we have the typical housewife who looks down on the working woman. She feels that a working woman becomes masculine by losing her feminine graces. She also accuses working housewives of neglecting their duties. This futile battle between working and non-working women is pointless. These dual roles should be complementary to each other. A woman should be given the liberty to choose what she thinks she can manage.

It is really enouraging to note that more women are in favour of women's employment than against it. It would be really worth investigating the other side of the picture by talking to men and other family members. If the social climate changes with families, particularly men favouring a career for women, women can be mobilised in larger numbers to participate in productive labour for their personal betterment and the welfare of society.

Why Women Take up Employment

Why do women want to work, however small the number? The factors which have been responsible for women's employment have been identified by a number of studies. According to the Labour Bureau's Report, four basic factors which have been responsible for women's employment, particularly the employment of mothers are: (*i*) permanent and growing inadequacy of the income of the principal bread winner; (*ii*) temporary fall in the family's income due to exceptional or accidental circumstances such as the sickness and premature incapacity of the principal earning member; (*iii*) the death of the bread winner; (*iv*) a woman's desire for economic independence or for securing a higher standard of living for the family.

The reasons are mainly economic in nature. A few other reasons for some housewives taking up employment may be explained in terms of individual talents, training, or interest in a particular job. Some wives work outside the home to use their free time or education or both. Still others work for personal satisfaction and individual development, and for some work gives social importance and a feeling of usefulness to the society at large.

Along with these there are certain situational characteristics of the family—the stage of the family life cycle, the presence or absence of children, age and sex of the children if present and the type of family—which might affect the employment of married women. Besides these, rapid social and cultural development also promote an increase in the labour force participation by married women.

The reason most frequently approved for married women to take employment seemed to be essentially economic in nature. Taking employment for financial support was approved of more often than for any other reason. Some of the other reasons were to avoid household routine, to enjoy outside contacts, to command respect from family members, to occupy time, to have freedom, to make use of education etc.

Effects of Employment of Married Women

Some of the most probable effects of the employment of a married woman would be her absence at meal times, inability to provide wholesome food or to entertain the husband's friends, failure to become a good cook or maintain an orderly home. Consequential effects would be that she is likely to become more independent, and she would be more prone to call upon the husband to share household work. The taking up of employment by the wife is visualised as leading to equalitarian power relationships.

The present investigation takes in view some differences between working wifes and a full-time housewife.

(*i*) The role in decision making is found to be almost the same for a working and non-working woman in a family, the percentage being slightly more for the working women.

(*ii*) Working wives prefer love marriages to arranged marriages.

(*iii*) There is a greater incidence of mixed marriages among working wives, than for the housewives.

(*iv*) Marital adjustment becomes more difficult for working wives.

(*v*) Husbands seem to be more understanding towards housewives as compared to working wives.

(*vi*) The husband's attitude towards relatives is more friendly in the case of housewives.

(*vii*) Working women generally prefer small families with one or two children, while housewives prefer families of medium size, i.e. three to four children.

Employment outside the home represents a major role-innovation for married women. This is apparently associated with some change in the traditional norms for the male-female division of role responsibilities. For instance, employment of wives should be associated with a decline in patriarchal authority patterns and with the emergence of equalitarian authority patterns. In the present investigations the respondents were asked about their say in matters like education of children, financial investment pattern, marriage of children etc. There was not much difference found between housewives and working wives as seen from the table.

Table 45

SAY IN FAMILY MATTERS ACCORDING TO THE
OCCUPATIONAL STATUS OF THE WIFE

Say in family matters	*Occupational status*			
	Housewives		*Working wives*	
	No.	*%*	*No.*	*%*
Never	45	6.97	16	7.88
Sometimes	323	50.00	93	45.81
Always	278	43.03	94	46.31
Total	646	100.00	203	100.00

But this again varies with the educational level of the life. If the wife is educated regardless of the fact whether she is a housewife or working wife, important decisions were made after consultation with her. Traditionally all decisions were made by the head of the family. With more and more education for women, some of the duties of the head of the family are transferred to the wife if she is competent enough to do the job. In previous researches done by investigators on decision making in families, the husband made decisions regarding money which was completely his domain. But with better education a syncratic cooperation of function evolved. Since in our sample about 40% of working wives have less than

primary education compared to about 25% of housewives with
that level of education, there is obviously not much difference between the two groups. But interviewing the middle group definitely
revealed some difference between the two group in terms of role
changes. Since the money was brought to the house by the women,
they commanded more respect, attention and consideration than
was customarily meted to women. Thus the increased economic
contribution of the employed wife to her family also may alter her
status and power relations with her spouse. In turn, the change
in the status of the spouse's may influence many spousal interaction
patterns.

Redefinition of husband and wife status positions and family
roles may be associated with increased spousal and intrapersonality
conflict. Major role innovations are frequently accompanied by
ambiguity and conflict when new and old definitions clash. The
employment of wives represents a deviation from one aspect of
the traditional husband-wife division of labour. It is not surprising
that women look more favourably upon role innovations associated
with their employment than do men. When we look at the picture
of household responsibilities shared by husband and wife in the
present study, there is surprisingly no difference between working
wives and housewives (Table 46).

Table 46

HUSBAND CO-OPERATING WITH HOUSEHOLD RESPONSIBILITIES
ACCORDING TO WIFE'S OCCUPATIONAL STATUS

| | Occupational status | | | |
| | Housewife | | Working wife | |
	No.	%	No.	%
Never	187	28.94	68	35.98
Sometimes	350	54.18	88	46.56
Often	109	16.88	33	17.46
Total	646	100.00	189	100.00

The figures here show a different picture than that of western
societies where the household work is shared by husband and wife
without any paid help. But in the Indian context, labour is comparatively cheap and with the addition of family income through
wife's employment working wives can afford to employ paid help

by which both the spouses are relieved of housework. Hence the question does not arise about husband's cooperation with household responsibilities. In the circumstances without any paid help, employed wives have less time available for home making roles. If the home-and-family-tasks which the wife did before her employment are done in as thorough a manner after her employment, she must expend more effort, become more efficient in these activities, or receive greater assistance from other family members or have paid help.

In the circumstances of wife being employed there are possible causes for husband-wife conflict. Further, discord may develop as adjustments in family roles and spousal status relations are required because of the employment of the wife. Adjustment of internal family roles might also be affected in which case the wife may be excused from participation in formal social organizations, or frequent visits to relatives.

Besides participating in decision making, or having a say in family matters, an employed wife was compared with a housewife regarding seeking advice from elders. Working wives tend to be confident about themselves and hence only slightly over 43% of them seek advice from elders, while over 60% housewives take advice from elders.

Table 47

SEEKING ADVICE FROM ELDERS ACCORDING TO OCCUPATIONAL STATUS

Response	*Occupational status*			
	Housewives		*Working wives*	
	No.	*%*	*No.*	*%*
Never	10	1.54	13	6.40
Sometimes	231	25.69	111	54.68
Always	405	62.77	79	38.92
Total	646	100.00	203	100.00

Further analysis revealed that the type which seeks advice are better adjusted in married life than those who do not. This might throw light on the adjustable nature of those who seek advice of which housewives are the majority.

NINE

Roles, Images, Ideals

Indian women have done and are still doing extraordinary things. History, literature, religion and politics abound with examples of women who have inspired others. Ironically, we have never made any attempt to understand the role, ideals and images of such extraordinarily dynamic personalities who have faced dire conseqences in their pursuit to benefit others, and derive satisfaction.

However, we are primarily concerned with the average Indian woman. What is her life, what is the image she wants to live up to, and what are her ideals? Our interest has been the present day woman and we have probed to find the attitude of such women to marriage, sexual freedom, dowry, family planning, women's education, employment, fashion, politics, and other vital issues.

As the sample covered a cross-section of urban women, the respondents were quite diverse. Despite the diversity it was possible to place the respondents into three distinct groups—the conservative, the liberal and the moderate, depending primarily on their education and social background. The cross-fertilisation of different ideas and customs has produced a uniformity in the social practices and beliefs of different provincial groups in the urban population making the area of origin less significant. For instance a typical middle class woman whether she is in the metropolis of Delhi or Bombay has similar problems and notions. An economically independent woman whether Calcutta-born or a Madrasi has a specific pattern of behaviour and a defined attitude to social norms. Mass media had also influenced habits and customs resulting in uniformity and a decrease in the cultural diversity of the urban population.

Caste influences were not considered as it does not affect women as much as men. The basis of caste being *varnashram* or occupation of a person, caste ceases to be a dynamic factor shaping the thinking and actions of urban people. They are more conditioned by their spending power, educational level and social standing than by caste. Even in rural areas a woman has no caste of her own, as she takes on that of her husband after marriage. The idea of caste is more flexible in the case of a woman. It influences her character, attitude and behaviour to a lesser degree. To whichever caste a woman may belong, she is primarily conditioned by her sex, her position as a wife, mother, and custodian of the house.

As caste and provincial attitudes are minimised, the socio-economic status, education, and to a lesser degree age, come up as the most important factors influencing woman's social behaviour. On some issues even these differences do not seem significant. Women have uniformly changed and have developed a positive approach irrespective of the numerous differences whether it be about the age of marriage, education of women, employment needs, family planning or dowry. On the other hand in spite of different environmental factors, women have demonstrated an unshakable conservatism about certain aspects of life. Progressive urban woman show increased awareness while conservatism is the outcome of a traditional upbringing.

India is still basically an agricultural country with just 20% living in the urban sector. Only a small percentage of those living in urban areas are conditioned by their mechanical living and preoccupations. The urban poor and often even the middle class are not completely urbanised as in the West. The effort of urbanisation has been significantly less on the Indian woman who is more traditional. In spite of modernisation, mechanisation, and the breaking up of the joint family, she has remained basically conservative. She has maintained her primary function as the preserver of the home and family whatever the upheavals in her personal life or changes in the environment.

FROM PASSIVITY TO ACTION

As we have observed in the introduction, though in theory the woman was the *grihalakshmi*, the goddess of the home, the image of the Mother Divine, her role has been denigrated through the centuries so that now she occupies a secondary status. Our traditional background, repeated foreign invasions and political unheavals, social rigidity, religious biogtry, were all responsible in suppressing the role of the Indian woman to that of subordinate status in the social structure.

The very foundation of a joint patriarchal family depended on the woman sacrificing her. She necessarily played a subservient role to man while he went out, earned and supported the family. She thus accepted a passive role, and believed that this secondary position was her true status. Marriage, maternity, lactation, the care of children and this exhausting cycle repeating itself throughout her life from adolescence to menopause physically incapacitated her and made her completely dependent on the male. Her passivity and lack of determination to face an unjust social structure kept her away from the mainstream of social change. She accepted discrimination without protest. If she lost her husband she even disfigured herself, willingly gave up wordly pleasures, and led a life of abstinence. If she could not bear a male child she was willing to take the place of a co-wife.

The last three decades have seen a remarkable change in woman's attitudes and the thoroughly domesticated, family-oriented Indian female has awakened from passivity to action. What has brought the change? A multiplicity of factors have affected the change. The foremost being the country's independence and a better deal for all, men and women. The social reforms in free India to ameliorate the social injustice to women were important in bringing an increased awareness about the discrimination which women had faced. The educational opportunities which women took advantage of set a new phase in social progress. The role of mass media in the education of the less informed and illiterate cannot be overlooked. Employment facilities with a variety of skilled, creative, administrative, and academic jobs available for women have also contributed to moderation. This led to economic emancipation in which women became as important as men in contributing to the family income, particularly in the lower level where the desire to take up employment was more a necessity than a choice. Family planning ushered a new era for the modern woman in every part of the world, more so for women in an economically-backward country like India. The better educated could now choose to limit their family size so that they could involve themselves in a multifaceted, all embracing role at home and in the country.

The modern Indian male's attitude to woman has also altered, and this has created a favourable climate for change in the status of women. Man had hitherto exploited the fact of woman's dependency, for his own good and for the betterment of his house and family, but today with his education, urban culture and dependence on his wife in a nuclear family he has undergone a tremendous change. The modern educated male is not satisfied with the prospect of a woman as a mere housewife. He wants an intelligent companion who will share his varied interests in life. Man has come to realise that a better position for women in society elevates the status of the entire household, family, and community. This change in the attitude of the Indian male has encouraged women to break the shackles of social discrimination.

Though a multitude of factors have influenced the great change that is noticed in women today, education has played the greatest role. The better a woman's education the greater the availability of social opportunities. When new opportunities come in, there is conflict with existing institutions. This leads to a change in thinking and in the pattern of living as indicated below.

EDUCATED WOMEN → HAS GREATER OPPORTUNI-
TIES → DESIRE TO EXPLOIT OPPORTUNITIES →
CHANGE IN ATTITUDE → CONFLICT WITH
EXISTING INSTITUTION → ACCEPTANCE OF NEW
CHALLENGES → WOMEN'S STATUS IMPROVES

Just as a child cannot perceive everything around him without being able to look through the window, an individual is unable to understand the facts of life if he does not have exposure to the outside world through education. Education alone can pave the path to positive attitudinal change and practices. The present study reveals that there is a significant change in women in attitudes towards inter-caste marriage, employment of married women, divorce, widow remarriage, family planning, co-education, sex education and girls' education because of increased education and economic development. Due to the change in thinking in the present era, attitudes towards marrying a widower or divorcee and attitude towards sex, premarital sex, sexual freedom for men and women etc. also have taken a different turn. Simultaneously a negative relationship is found between education and the attitude towards dowry, religion and the joint family system (Fig. 29).

The age for marriage is not only increased with the advancement of education, but is even thought to be the ideal one. Married life has better chances of happiness with college level education, since the chances decrease with advanced studies and specialisation. Inter-caste marriage, sex knowledge, courtship, free mixing, and practice of family planning are ideas which have been favourably conditioned by education. Employment opportunities are increased with better educational qualifications. Those who are better educated seek employment also.

Interactional problems and hence differences of opinion with parents increase with education. Thus the generation gap gets wider. Fashion consciousness with preference for unconventional clothes, smoking, drinking, use of tranquillisers etc. are all influenced to a certain extent by education. Socio-economic status also influences these practices to a great extent. Interactional problems are found more in the upper socio-economic strata. Restrictions are imposed on girls of the lower strata while upper class girls have a liberal upbringing and are less inclined to abide by the wishes of their parents.

Recreational habits like reading, playing etc. are rare among women of the lower socio-economic strata. But in the practice of smoking the lower strata outweigh the middle one. The lower socio-economic group are more interested in cooking. In the attitude towards dowry or marrying a divorcee, the lower group is more favourable than the upper or middle group.

The Indian woman though conditioned by tradition, custom, public opinion and religious beliefs is showing a remarkable change as a result of education. Whether a typical housewife or a working woman or a combination of both, women today have acquired a multitude of new functions while retaining quite a few old ones. The change in woman has been remarkable though not revolutionary. It is good that she has not undergone a revolutionary change. This would have had the disadvantage of uprooting tested values and practices without offering a workable substitute.

WOMEN, SEX AND MARRIAGE

We have observed that the Indian woman even today is conservative about certain aspects of life in spite of her living in an urban culture. She is conservative in her ideas about marriage, divorce, and widow marriage. Her moderation in fashion and her aversion to drinks and drugs throw light on her cautious mental make up. For the great majority religion plays a major role and exerts a strong influence on their character and mental stability.

Even regarding sex norms the normal woman shows an inflexibility. She takes for granted that her sex norms have to be different from that of the male. She is convinced her attitude of sexual restraint outside the marital relationship has preserved the sanctity of the marriage partnership. She abhors the sexual permissiveness rampant in so called "progressive" sections of society which is a parody of the western attitude towards sex. She has no intention of following these footsteps. Our cultural background is such that the average woman does not consider herself mainly an object of man's lust.

Though marriage is a personal necessity, women in India regard it as a societal obligation and not merely a personal relationship. It is seen that good marital adjustment is found with a combination of situational factors like socio-economic status, occupational status, educational status, sexual and temperamental compatibility and other factors like comparable family background, co-operation from in-laws, syncratic co-operation of husband and wife, and above all if women are determined to make marriage a success. Because the focus is more on what is good for others than for one's own individual needs, Indian women make a success of their marriage in the majority of instances whatever be the environmental factors.

HOME AND THE FAMILY

Whatever the upheavals in life, the Indian woman knows a stable family gives her security from which she derives emotional strength. Before marriage she is attached to her parental home and avoids confrontation with her parents. She maintains loyalty for her parental home even after years of marriage. Once married she recognises the mutual dependency of the husband and wife. Many of them, even the unsophisticated, know they are as indispensable to their husbands as their husbands are to them. Harmony between family members and a stable home is the basis of her

happiness. Even in nuclear homes the tendency is to retain con-
nections with the larger family. Family get-togethers during
vacations, festivals, marriages, anniversaries, house-warmings and
births are a part of the average Indian household even today.
Women perpetuate these customs and practices. Family interdependence is the basis of the strength of the Indian famlly.

WOMEN AND WORK

In a modern urban setup more amenities are available to ease the
domestic work load. As such women cannot remain merely
housewives especially when the family is small. The more enlightened women step out of domesticity to play an active part in society.

However, for an average woman to think of a role other than a
housewife is a new proposition. She doubts her ability to effectively
manage home and work, more so if the husband is uncooperative
and the family background antagonistic. Besides, many women
who wish to take up employment do not wish to do so at the risk
of neglecting their domestic responsibilities.

Even among highly educated career oriented women their consideration for the house and family often takes priority over their
professional obligations, especially when the children are small and
need the attention of the mother.

The hand to mouth existence of the poor often makes it impera-
tive that the women work to supplement the family income. The
economic battle reduces every other consideration to a secondary
level as many of them have been severely uprooted from their life
in the villages. They willingly accept employment out of sheer
necessity not choice. If given the choice woman would give
primary inportance to the domestic role.

The average woman rich or poor is unable to relinquish her
duties as mother and wife whatever her role or economic status.
Her attitude to work has however changed, and she no more
considers taking employment outside the domestic sphere as
unfeminine. If she does not work it is either because of her
domestic responsibilities, her insufficiency, or certain adverse
environmental factors. Even women of the older generation from
all stratas understand that a woman's income helps the family.

The data revealed that more than 70% of women are favourable
towards employment regardless of their status, but environmental

forces often act as a deterrant. Many times girls are considered as articles to be disposed off as quickly as possible without even giving the appropriate training for them to become mature, responsible citizens to assume the responsibility of any kind of career or even parenthood in this present age. Once the child bearing period is over, many women feel useless which in turn has a detrimental effect on their physical and mental health. Besides, the standards of living of a developing nation like India will not improve unless women participate in developmental efforts. Hence emphasis by authorities on job oriented education for girls in both villages and cities is essential.

In underdeveloped countries it is surprising to note that there is surplus labour and it becomes difficult to utilise it. This is true of women who do not utilise time, energy or training effectively. If only a national programme could be chalked out to relieve woman during the child bearing period and later enable her to return to work, then only could an efficient use of her resources be achieved.

Negative Approach to Work

Some Indian women have a positively unfavourable attitude to work. The poor, illiterate woman who has limited resources and opportunities seems to be unable to help herself about anything. She refuses to change, avail of opportunities and take up challenges. The newly rich feel it is their privilege to live a life of indolence. The so called modern rich women who waste their time in manicuring and hair setting, playing cards and attending social get-togethers have all the time and opportunities which they refuse to exploit. It is such women who have freedom from domestic chores because of the availability of servants. They have no regard for anything Indian and blindly ape the west in the name of being progressive. It is unfortunate that such women have not taken a positive approach to work to make their contribution to society.

Every woman must be a worker, contributing to society in a large or small measure. Women have to psychologically prepare themselves to be more effective members of society. Every woman who has the privilege of education must be willing to rough it out if necessary to share with man the task of shaping society. This alone will remove the stigma of dependency attached to her and ensure respect and dignity.

WOMAN'S EQUALITY

For the average woman, the question of equality with man is something she has never bothered about, as she happily accepts her domestic role. When the necessity arises or when time is available she takes up employment and there the question ends. Even the educated woman who hears the fuss being made to equate woman with man is surprised that woman should want to make this claim. As a young artist put it, "Can man claim equality with woman? No." Whatever may be said to prove the equality of the sexes, one cannot deny the fact that in the biological sense woman has a greater role and responsibility. Man is not geared to woman in this sense. The burden of maternity, childbirth and childcare cannot be lessened even if the family is small with just two or three children. A fair slice of a woman's productive age between 20-35 (even with family planning) is taken up by her duties as a mother. However, the Indian woman realises it to be to her advantage if she accepts this instead of considering it a burden.

Modern urban society lays great stress on the individual. Till the wave of industrialisation overtook the lives of men and women, the focus was on the family, home and society. Now woman is waking up to her rights as an individual, and especially to the issue of economic independence. Indeed the women's liberation movement in the west is living on the issue of economic equality.

The Indian woman is not belligerent in waging a battle on the economic front. She is more worried about social discrimination, and the question as to who is more powerful or important never comes up. Woman happily accepts her role, though economically she contributes less than man. If woman is economically dependent on man, man is emotionally dependent on the woman who gives him a happy, stable home.

THE CHANGE

Though till now the stereotyped feminine role has secured as a pattern of conduct, the present decade is significant in that it will decide how much of the traditional practices will be retained and how much rejected. A great wave of social change is overtaking the country with numerous social laws in favour of women. At no time in the history of the nation has such a positive, all-out effort been taken to raise the status of woman. It is only the educated woman in a better economic status who can think about these new changes and set the pace for a social renaissance. What can be done for women who are underprivileged, exploited and discarded, who constitute a large proportion of Indian women? While the educated, especially from the better strata of society have taken full advantage of all opportunities available, these unfortunate women have remained uncomplaining though subjected to humiliation and disrespect on account of their sex. Our hearts go out to Archana, a 12 year old victim of child marriage, Seeta the young Brahmin widow with shaven head who has faced social ostracism from the age of 20, and Shantibai who ran away from home unable to bear the cruelty of her husband and ended as a postitute in the streets of Bombay, Vimalaji humiliated and degraded to the status of a co-wife after 15 years of marriage because she could not bear a son.

These are living examples of females who live and die under the evil of child marriage, widowhood, dowry and polygamy. What can be done to bring a consciousness in these women to improve their own lot?

The problem of social awakening for women has to be tackled by an integrated effort. Our efforts should be to implement these changes as quickly as possible. A decade to bring about this awakening may be a short period in the life of a nation but not for the individual oppressed by the unjust practices of a conservative and tradition-bound society.

We should focus our attention on socially underprivileged women providing them education and employment opportunities, knowledge of family planning, and social privileges which at present are only theoretical.

Education and Family Planning

Change through formalised education is a gradual process. We cannot educate overnight the 150 million adult women scattered throughout India. The form of education should be subtle indoctrination to make women realise their important status at home and in the community. They must know their privileges. Mass media should be oriented to uplifting the urban and rural poor. For the women belonging to the social elite it has to be a reeducation so that they see good in the time-tested cultural and tradition-

202 Indian Women Today

al institutions which are the basis of a stable society.

An all out effort must be made to educate women on famliy planning. A woman must be given the choice to limit her family depending on her health, availability of time, and economic status. Though family planning is essential, compulsion of any sort should be totally avoided. For Indian women, be they Hindus, Jains, Christians or Muslims, the maternal role is of primary importance. Enforced compulsory family planning unfortunately does not take into account ecology, demography, human psychology and genetics; and the long term effects are ignored in our concern for immediate results.

Employment Opportunities

Employment opportunities to help women do not mean that men and women will necessarily do the same type of jobs and get into cut-throat competition. Men and women must learn to respect each other's work to nurture a healthier atmosphere in society. The focus should be to utilise women's capabilities and potentialities to facilitate a social and cultural renaissance than to throw them against men to fight an indiscriminate economic battle.

Women must be provided part-time jobs in different fields so that they are able to work without seriously upsetting their domestic responsibilities. As many working women interrupt their career in order to fulfil their duties to the home and children, they must be given the opportunity to recontinue their career after the lapse of the years spent at home as wife and mother. This means many women will have two phases of work in their career, one before marriage and the other after the children are a little older and domestic responsibilities fewer. As yet Indian working women are not yet ready to entrust the upbringing of their children completely to day-care institutions.

Social Awareness

Social reforms and laws alone do not bring a change. The change must be effected in the minds of men and women, whether it is widow remarriage, intercaste marriage, marriage without dowry, women's employment or woman's participation in decision-making. All these involve a social awakening in both men and women.

The backward, conservative woman herself is often the greatest obstacle to social change. She is conditioned to think that to be a woman is unfortunate, she curses her stars when a girl is born, she supports the dowry system to increase her riches, supports child marriage as the best way to keep girls from going astray, and insists on the "ghoonghat" to preserve chastity. The negative attitude of such women to social change is a great hurdle to reckon with, and every educated woman should enlighten her less priviledged conservative sisters. It is an uphill task, but has to be tackled effectively through individual efforts.

A change in outlook should come in men also if woman has to contribute more to the community and society. There are innumerable instances where men object to a woman working even if she has the time, energy and capability. There are other examples where women are treated as chattels to serve every whim and fancy of the male. Man should respect woman not for what she does for him, but as an individual with the right to think and act according to her own conviction.

INDIAN WOMEN TODAY

The educated woman has realised she cannot remain confined to the four walls of her home if she has to play her multifaceted role, for she must be progressive enough to accept the new challenges and social changes overtaking the country. She realises she is on level with man, his equal and not his subordinate. In fact the Indian woman is moving towards an ideal balance of traditional and progressive values.

Though basically religious, women today give less importance to temple-going, rituals, and superstitions. Orthodox practices have become less significant in the face of progressive urban culture. The maturity of character the woman displays whatever her social status, upbringing or educational level is due to her deep conviction of her own importance for the home and the happiness of the family. This conviction has been handed down to her as part of her cultural heritage. She looks down on the so called modern liberated females who have lost their very identity in their pursuit for liberation. The new Indian woman wants to retain her intrinsic love for the home, the children and the family and combine with this her determination to play a vital role in the socio-economic structure of modern India.

Bibliography

AGARWAL, A.K., "Liberal Divorce Laws: Will They Aggravate Marital Problems?" *Eve's Weekly*, 28 June 1975.

ALTEKAR, A. S., *The Position of Women in Hindu Civilization*, Motilal Banarsidas Publishers, Banaras, 1956.

Anthropology Department, Calcutta University, "Attitude of Calcutta College Girls Towards Marriage," Calcutta, Unpublished Research, 1976.

BAIG, TARA ALI, *Women of India*, New Delhi, Publications Division, Government of India, 1958.

BECKER, HOWARD, and HILL, REUBEN, *Marriage and the Family*, D.C. Heath and Company, Boston, 1942.

——*Family, Marriage and Parenthood*, D. C. Heath and Company, Boston, 1948.

BELL, W. NORMAN and VOGEL, EZRA, *A Modern Introduction to the Family*, Macmillan Limited, New York, 1960.

BHASIN, KAMALA, "The Position of Women in India." Proceedings of a seminar held in Srinagar, Orient House, Bombay, 1972.

BUCK, PEARL, *Of Men and Women*, Doubleday and Co. Inc., New York, 1941.

CHRISTENSEN, H. T., *Marriage Analysis, Foundations for Successful Family Life*, Ronald Press Co., New York, 1950.

CORMACK, MARGARET, *The Hindu Women*, Asia Publishing House, Bombay, 1961.

DAVID, OPAL D., *The Education of Women, Signs for the Future*, American Council on Education, Washington D. C., 1959.

DAVIS, KINGSLEY, "The Sociology of Parent Youth Conflict," *American Sociological Review 4*, 1940, pp. 423-435.

DESAI, NEERA, *Women in Modern India*, Vora and Co. Publishers Private Ltd., Bombay, 1957.

DUBE, S. C., *Men's and Women's Roles in India, Women in the New Asia*, United Nations Educational Scientific and Cultural Organisation, Paris, 1963.

DUMONT, RENE, "Women's Role in Development," *International Labour Review*, vol. 3:6, 1975.

EPSTEIN, CYNTHIA, *Woman's Place, Options and Limits in Professional Careers*, University of California Press, California, 1973.

EPSTEIN, JOSEPH, *Divorced in America: Marriage in an Age of Possibility*, E. P. Dutton & Co., New York, 1974.

FARBER, SEYMOUR M., and ROGER, H. L. WILSON, *The Potential of Women*, McGrawHill Paper Backs, New York, 1963.

FOOTE, NELSON, "New Roles for Men and Women," *Marriage and Family Living*, 23:4, 1961, pp. 325-329.

FRIEDAN, BETTY, *The Feminine Mystique*, W. W. Norton and Co., New York, 1963.

GOODE, WILLIAM J., *The Family*, Prentice Hall of India Ltd., New Delhi, 1965.

GREER, GERMAINE, *Female Eunuch*, Macgibbon v Kee, 1970.

HATE, C. A., *Hindu Woman and her Future*, New Book Co., Bombay, 1963.

India, Ministry of Labour and Employment, Labour Bureau Pamphlet Series No. 8, 1-59, 1964.

India 1971-72, Research and Reference Division of the Ministry of Information and Broadcasting, 1972.

International Labour Organisation, Female earnings as percentage of male earnings in agricultural employment in selected countries, Geneva, 1971.

KANNAN, C.T., *Intercaste and Intercommunity Marriages in India*, Allied Publishers Private Ltd., Bombay, 1963.

KAPADIA, K. M., *Marriage and Family in India*, 3rd ed., Oxford University Press, Bombay, 1966.

KAPUR, PROMILLA, *Marriage and the Working Woman in India*, Vikas Publications, New Delhi, 1970.

——*The Changing Status of the Working Woman in India*, Vikas Publications, New Delhi, 1974.

——*Love, Marriage, Sex and the Indian Woman*, Orient Paperbacks, New Delhi, 1976.

KINSEY, ALFRED et al., *Sexual Behaviour of the Human Female*, W.B. Saunders Co., Philadelphia, 1953.

KIRKPATRICK, JEANE J., *Political Woman*, Basic Books Inc. Publishers, New York, 1974.

KLEEN, VIOLA, *The Feminine Character*, 2nd ed., Routledge Kegan Paul Ltd., London, 1971.

KOMAROVSKY, MIRRA, *Women in the Modern World—Their Education and their Dilemmas*, Houghton Miffin Co., Boston, 1953.

KOMAROVSKY, MIRRA (ed.), *The Functional Analysis of Sex Roles in Marwin Sussman, Source Book an Marriage and the Family*, Houghton Miffin Co., Boston, 3rd ed., 1968.

KUPPUSWAMY, B., *Manual of Socio Economic Status Scale* (Urban), Manasayan, Delhi, 1962.

MACCOBY, ELEANOR, (ed.), *The Development of Sex Differences*, Stanford University Press, Stanford California, 1966.

MADHOK, UMA, "Indian Women in a Changing Society," *Journal of Social Welfare*, 15:25-27, 1967.

MANNILA, E. M., "Sex Differentiation in Role Expectations and Performance," *Journal of Marriage and the Family*, 29:568-578, 1967.

MISRA, B. B., *Indian Middle Classes—Their Growth in Modern Times*, Oxford University Press, India, 1961.

MUKHERJEE, RADHA KAMAL, *The Horizon of Marriage*, Asia Publishing House, Bombay, 1957.

MYRDAL, ALVA, AND KLEIN, VIOLA, *Women's Two Roles*, Routledge and Kegan Paul Ltd., London, 1956.

National Council of Applied Economic Research, *All India Household Survey of Income, Saving and Consumer Expenditure*, New Delhi, NCAER, 1972.

NATH, K., "Women in the Working Force in India," *Economic and Political Weekly*, Sameksha Trust Publication No. 31, 1205-1215, 1968.

PANDEY, KANTI, "Distressing Conditions of Female Farm Workers," *Economic Times*, 11 May 1975.

PRAKASH, PADMA, "Urban Women," *Eve's Weekly*, 20 September 1975, pp. 10-11.

PRITCHARD, E. E. Evans, *The Persuasion of Women in Primitive Society*, Faber, London, 1965.

REID, ELIZABETH, "Women at a Standstill," *International Labour Review*, 3-6, 1975.

ROSS, A. D., *The Hindu Family in its Urban Setting*, Oxford University Press, India, 1961.

SASTRI, SAKUNTALA RAO, *Women in the Sacred Law*, Bharatiya Vidya Bhavan, Bombay, 1952.

SEN GUPTA, SANKAR, *Women in Indian Folklore—Linguistic and Religious Study, A short survey of their social status and position*, Indian Folklore Society, Indian Publication, Calcutta, 1969.

——*A Study of Women of Bengal*, Indian Publication, Calcutta, 1970.

SRINIVAS, M. N., *Social Change in Modern India*, University of California Press, Berkely, Los Angeles, 1971.

STASSINOPOULAUS, ARIANNA, *The Female Woman*, Glasgow, Fontana-Collins, 1974.

The Times of India Directory & Year Book, New Delhi, The Times of India Press, 1976.

TYLER, LEONA E., *Psychology of Human Differences*, 3rd ed., Vakils, Feffer and Simons Private Ltd., Bombay, 1969.

Index